West Acad

Emeritus Advisory Board

West Academic Publishing's Law School Advisory Board

a short & happy guide to

Administrative Law

Second Edition

William D. Araiza
Stanley A. August Professor of Law
Brooklyn Law School

A SHORT & HAPPY GUIDE® SERIES

WEST
ACADEMIC
PUBLISHING

© 2018 LEG, Inc. d/b/a West Academic
© 2022 LEG, Inc. d/b/a West Academic
      444 Cedar Street, Suite 700
      St. Paul, MN 55101
      1-877-888-1330
Printed in the United States of America

ISBN: 978-1-63659-261-9

To my students over the years.

Acknowledgments

Professor Araiza thanks Andrey Udalov for very helpful assistance in preparing the First Edition of this book and Parker Brown and Derek Knight for equally helpful assistance in preparing the Second Edition.

Table of Contents

A Short & Happy Guide to Administrative Law

Second Edition

Introduction

Administrative law is like air—it's invisible but all around us. It's invisible (at least to the uninitiated) because when we read about the latest anti-pollution regulation from the Environmental Protection Agency or the latest enforcement action against an investment firm by the Securities and Exchange Commission, we read, talk, and debate about the substance of the action: whether the regulation is well thought-out or the enforcement action properly aggressive or too little, too late. What we normally don't talk about—unless it's an unusual situation—is the administrative process that led to that decision. That process—the stuff of administrative law—is thus often invisible. But it's also all around us, because that regulation and enforcement action—as well as everything else any agency does—is governed by law that dictates the process the agency must follow and the type of scrutiny that decision will receive if and when it is challenged in court.

Because administrative law permeates government action (since most of such action is in fact performed by agencies), understanding administrative law is crucial. Whether you want to practice in environmental, securities, immigration, or almost any other area of law, you need to understand the processes governing agency action. Even seemingly common law-governed areas require an understanding of administrative law. For example, if you want to be a real estate lawyer, you'll have to deal with land-use regulations promulgated by zoning commissions and appear in front of such commissions for variances (which in some ways are just another type of administrative adjudication).

But you probably already know all this, because you're already signed up for administrative law. So let's get started with the process of understanding it.

This *Guide*—and probably the course you're taking—focuses on federal administrative law. That's not because federal administrative law is the only game in town. Far from it: as the zoning commission example above makes clear, states and even sub-units of states have their own sets of administrative procedures. But most introductory courses in administrative law focus on federal law, just like most introductory civil procedure classes focus on federal civil procedure and most introductory evidence classes focus on the Federal Rules of Evidence. In the case of administrative law, that's because, often, the most developed jurisprudence of administrative law exists at the federal level. But the good news is that the principles of administrative law you'll learn in your federal law class generally transfer, if imprecisely, to most state law systems. To be sure, variations exist between states and the federal government and among the states themselves. But the basics are just that—pretty basic and fairly standard.

So, what exactly *is* administrative law? At the risk of oversimplifying, it's the law that governs "the administrative state"—the term judges and scholars use to describe the sprawling bureaucracy that governs so much of our daily lives, from the food that we eat (regulated for safety by the Food and Drug Administration) to the cars that we drive (regulated for safety by the National Highway Transportation Safety Administration and for emissions by the Environmental Protection Agency) to the investments we make (regulated by the Securities and Exchange Commission), and nearly everything in between.

Note one important thing, though: administrative law does not speak to the substantive law governing any particular regulatory area. Thus, this is not a class where you'll learn about federal food safety, automotive safety, environmental, or securities law. To be sure, you'll read cases dealing with those areas, but only because those cases announce or apply rules of administrative law. To repeat, administrative law is the law that governs the agencies that regulate us—not that regulatory law itself.

But this is still a lot—an awful lot. Administrative law, like the administrative state, is a sprawling topic. Most classes begin (as does this *Guide*) by considering the constitutional status of the administrative state. This material may seem theoretical, but it's very important. The administrative state sits in an awkward position in our federal governmental system (and, indeed, the system of each state government as well). As you probably have already learned, the federal system contemplates a legislature that makes law, an executive that enforces the law, and a judiciary that interprets the law and applies it in particular cases. Agencies, however, do all three of these jobs. As you'll see in Part Two of this *Guide*, they promulgate regulations that look a lot like statutes. As you'll see in Part Three, they also adjudicate violations of the federal laws they're empowered to administer. They also prosecute those violations.

There's good reason for this combination of functions. Today, effective regulation requires a degree of detail and expertise that is simply beyond the capacity of Congress. For example, the Environmental Protection Agency has to promulgate extremely detailed regulations governing air and water quality standards. Even if Congress had the inclination to perform that minute level of regulation, it would not have the technical expertise to do so—nor would it have the time to keep those regulations up-to-date in light of changing knowledge. Similarly, agency adjudicators (called "administrative law judges" or "ALJs") have the detailed knowledge of the particular issues they review that allows them to make accurate rulings, even if those rulings are usually appealable to an Article III federal court.

Nevertheless, combining all these functions in one institution creates a great deal of tension with our traditional preference for separating, rather than combining, governmental powers. This problem is exacerbated by the fact that Congress has made some agencies "independent" of presidential control, by immunizing the heads of those agencies from the risk of presidential removal for policy disagreements. This phenomenon creates the specter of administrative agencies that are not fully accountable to the President, Congress, or the courts—what commentators have described as a "headless fourth branch of government." The Supreme Court has attempted to preserve the best of this system of combined powers and agency independence, while avoiding its most troubling aspects, in a set of cases we'll consider in Part One.

Part Two considers the process by which agencies promulgate regulations. That part introduces you to the Administrative Procedure Act (APA). The APA is a crucial statute for administrative law and administrative law students; indeed, it's not an exaggeration to say that it's the foundational statute for our entire regulatory system. As important as it is, it may be surprising for you to learn that the APA was only enacted in 1946. But that late date becomes more understandable once you remember that it was only in the 1930s, with Franklin Roosevelt's New Deal, that federal regulation became as prevalent as it is today. (Of course, it's only grown since then.) That's not to say there was no federal regulation before the 1930s. There was: there was already a food inspection system, a radio regulation system, a national currency regulated by the Federal Reserve Board, and a whole host of other regulatory institutions. But the growth of federal regulation during the 1930s convinced many that a uniform law was needed to govern the process by which agencies regulate. That's what the APA is.

Part Two considers what the APA says about the rulemaking process. Rulemaking is one of the fundamental ways by which agencies act. Essentially, regulations—the product of the rulemaking process—are like statutes. They impose generally-applicable and (usually) prospective requirements: for example, the EPA might impose a requirement that all automobiles must run on clean-burning gasoline that's less harmful to the environment. By contrast, the other fundamental way an agency acts—by adjudicating—is akin to judicial action. Adjudications generally involve one subject (the target, or "defendant," of an agency "enforcement action"), based on conduct that has already occurred. While the difference between rulemaking and adjudication sounds straightforward (and often is), that isn't always the case. Part Two begins by considering that distinction, and then considering the discretion agencies possess to employ one of these vehicles or the other.

The rest of Part Two considers the rulemaking process. Of course, the EPA can't just promulgate regulations because it feels like it: rather, it can only act under the authority Congress gives it— in this case, when Congress enacted the Clean Air Act. As you'll see in Part Two, the APA provides the process by which agencies such as the EPA promulgate these regulations. You'll see that there's an informal process (also called the notice-and-comment process, for reasons you'll see in Part Two) and a more formalized process. You'll also see that the APA exempts certain types of rules from some or all of these procedural requirements. Part Two will also consider issues of integrity in rulemaking—in particular, the problems posed when agency personnel engaged in a rulemaking conduct *ex parte*, private, off-the-record communications about the issues in that rulemaking, and when those personnel are alleged to have pre-judged the issues that are the subject of the rulemaking process. Part Two concludes by considering attempts presidents have made over the last several decades to control the rulemaking process more directly.

Part Three considers agency adjudication. As noted above, agency adjudication is akin to its judicial cousin, in that it's targeted at one subject and based on conduct that's already occurred. The APA says a great deal about what has to happen when Congress mandates that an agency use a formal process to adjudicate; Part Three will discuss those requirements. But the APA says surprisingly little about *informal* adjudications. Instead, the law governing informal agency adjudication is, for the most part, the law provided by the Due Process Clauses of the Fifth Amendment (applicable to the federal government) and the Fourteenth Amendment (applicable to the states). After discussing the APA's requirements for formal adjudication, Part Three then considers what the Due Process Clauses of these amendments require. Part Three then considers the same integrity concerns—about *ex parte* communications and bias—that Part Two considered in the rulemaking context. Indeed, the discussion of integrity issues in adjudications will refer you back to the analogous chapter in the rulemaking Part of this *Guide*, as some APA integrity rules apply equally to rulemaking and adjudication.

That's it for the process. But that's not it for the subject—not by a long shot. A crucial part of administrative law consists of judicial review of agency action—when and under what conditions such review is available, and what it looks like. Part Four examines the availability question. As you'll see, the APA speaks voluminously about whether, how, and when judicial review is available, and at the behest of which types of parties. Part Four considers all of these issues. As you'll see, the APA often provides very generous provisions for judicial review. Nevertheless, it still imposes important limits. In addition, the Supreme Court has decided that some limits on the availability of judicial review are imposed by the Constitution itself—in particular, Article III's creation of a federal court system with the power to hear only "cases and controversies." Part Four will consider both what the APA says about the availability of judicial review, and what the Constitution says.

Part Five considers what that judicial review looks like. As you'll see, Part Five divides its examination of this topic by the type of agency function the court is reviewing: agency fact-finding, agency interpretation of law, and something called agency "policy-making." As you can imagine, agencies find lots of facts. An agency doing a rulemaking on climate change will have to find the facts about the pace of climate change and the most effective ways of mitigating it. An agency doing an adjudication against a particular party will, of course, find facts about that particular party's conduct. Given that agencies are experts in the areas in which they operate, it shouldn't surprise you that courts will often defer to an agency's fact-findings.

Agencies also interpret law. For example, when promulgating an air pollution regulation the EPA will have to interpret the Clean Air Act in order to determine what requirements, if any, Congress specified for the particular pollution issue the agency is considering. It might surprise you to learn that, despite courts' insistence on their unique role in interpreting federal law, they often defer to an agency's reading of the statute it is implementing.

Finally, agencies engage in "policy-making." Part Five will explain what this term means, but for now suffice it to say that it involves the agency's combination of facts and law to reach a regulatory result. Many of the most important cases dealing with agency action involve judicial review of such policy-making.

Part Five will consider how courts review agencies' performance of each of these functions.

Part Six concludes the *Guide*, by discussing agencies and information. As you probably already realize, in the modern era information is crucial to power. Agencies have lots of information, and have lots of power to compel private parties to turn such information over, for example, via a subpoena for business records. Conversely, though, federal law, in particular the Freedom of Information Act (FOIA), requires agencies to disclose an enormous amount of the information they possess, upon request from a private party. Part Six considers, in turn, agencies' ability to acquire information, and their obligations under FOIA to disclose information.

Four final points before we start engaging the material. First, this *Guide* focuses an enormous amount on the APA. That's appropriate—after all, the APA is the default statute that governs agency procedures (rulemaking and adjudication), and the availability and content of judicial review of agency action. But note—it's just a default. Congress, if it wishes, can always prescribe different procedures and different judicial review rules in the course of writing a particular statute, such as the Clean Air Act or the Securities and Exchange Act. This *Guide* refers to such laws as the agency's "organic statute"—that is, the statute that gives the agency the power to act to begin with. Because the organic statute can always supersede the APA's requirements, it's critical to your job as a lawyer always to consult not just the APA, but the organic statute that empowers the agency with which you're dealing.

Second, a note about the organization of this *Guide*, and how it might relate to the organization of your course. This *Guide* follows a very conventional organizational sequence. But it's not the only one professors use when they teach. There are lots of ways to teach administrative law, and you should be aware of how the organization of your course's syllabus might differ from the organization of this *Guide*. This *Guide* tries to make that job easier, by providing intuitive and self-explanatory Part and Chapter headings.

Third, *read the statute and the cases*. This *Guide* is designed to provide a short (and happy) overview of the most important topics in administrative law. But it's no substitute for doing the hard work of slogging through the APA and the cases your professor assigns. Use this *Guide* as a complement to that reading, to illustrate ideas that otherwise seem unclear after you've struggled with your required course reading. But don't use it as a replacement for that reading.

Fourth, consider tracking what you learn in this class with the actions of a particular agency. Administrative law can seem very abstract, and, for that reason, difficult to grasp. If you happen to be taking a class in a heavily regulated area at the same time you're taking this class, try to map what you're learning here onto the agency actions you're studying in the other class. For example, if you're taking Securities Law while you're taking Administrative Law, try to make sense of the Securities and Exchange Commission's (SEC's) actions based on what you're learning. Is the SEC promulgating a regulation or bringing an enforcement action? Is the agency adjudicating that enforcement action? How are challengers getting into court to challenge an SEC action, and what type of review is the court performing?

If you're not taking a class like that while you're taking Administrative Law, then consider getting to know a particular agency's website, maybe the website of the agency that regulates an area in which you're interested. For example, if you're interested in environmental law, get on epa.gov and poke around.

You'll find tabs that explain the agency's existing and proposed regulations, set forth the agency's policy statements, and, in general, explain what the agency is up to.

Either of these approaches can help provide you with a factual context for what, again, can sometimes seem like abstract procedural requirements. Of course, you're just starting to learn about administrative law, so don't be surprised if you encounter items or agency conduct you don't understand. If you do, ask your professor; between the two of you, you can figure out what that seemingly-mysterious agency action is really all about.

Enough preliminaries. Here we go.

PART ONE

The Constitutional Status of Administrative Agencies

There is a lot about the structure of federal administrative agencies (what is sometimes referred to as "the administrative state") that doesn't easily fit within our intuitions about the type of government established by the Constitution in 1787. Most obviously, agencies aren't even mentioned in the Constitution, and are thus not authorized to wield any of the power "We the People" "vested" in Congress, the President, and the Article III judiciary. Yet agencies existed from the very start of the Republic. That's for a good reason: even in 1789 it was clear that the power to accomplish some tasks had to be lodged, or "vested," in a government official who was not a congressperson, the President, or a federal judge. Indeed, the Constitution contemplated the existence of such officials, given Article II's provision about which officials could be appointed by the President ("Officers of the United States") and which could be appointed by "the Courts of Law," the "Heads of Departments," or the President ("inferior officers"). U.S. Const., Art. II, § 2, cl. 2.

Ever since then questions have arisen about which powers could be vested in such officials, and what level of control the President and Congress could have over them.

CHAPTER 1

The Non-Delegation Doctrine

Many administrative law courses begin their examination of the constitutional status of administrative agencies with the non-delegation doctrine. The non-delegation doctrine considers what limits, if any, the Constitution places on Congress's power to give agencies power to promulgate regulations. The theoretical foundations of the doctrine rest in the first sentence of Article I of the Constitution: "All legislative powers herein granted shall be vested in a Congress of the United States . . . ." The "herein granted" part refers to the rest of Article I (and, ultimately, to other parts of the Constitution, such as Congress's power to enforce the Fourteenth Amendment). Thus, that phrase encompasses issues you may have studied in Constitutional Law, such as Congress's power to regulate interstate commerce. For our purposes, the key part of this sentence is the so-called "vesting" clause, which "vests" all the legislative powers granted to the federal government in the newly-created Congress. The theory of the non-delegation doctrine is that, since "We the People" vested these powers in Congress, Congress cannot turn around and hand those powers off (*i.e.*, delegate them) to another body, such as an administrative agency. Hence the "non-delegation" doctrine.

Beyond the text of Article I, the non-delegation requirement has been thought to provide important benefits to American government. First, it is defended as a way of ensuring that important policy decisions are made by the people's representatives in Congress, rather than by unelected bureaucrats. Second, it has been thought to ensure that a standard exists by which courts can ensure that agencies remain within legal boundaries—without a non-delegation principle, it has been reasoned, Congress could authorize agencies to legislate as they (the agencies) pleased, with no statutory limits and thus no limits that could be enforced by a reviewing court.

Despite this theory and these justifications for a non-delegation principle, it was clear from the start of the Republic that some decisions that could be described as "legislative" had to be delegated to administrative officials. Starting in the early nineteenth century, the Supreme Court uniformly upheld such delegations, using a variety of doctrinal formulas to guide the Court's decision. In the 1928 case of *J.W. Hampton v. United States*, 276 U.S. 394 (1928), the Court announced that the relevant question in non-delegation cases was whether Congress, in the statute authorizing the agency action, had articulated "an intelligible principle" that could serve to guide the agency's action. Ever since 1928, the so-called "intelligible principle" doctrine has governed non-delegation challenges.

The Court has invoked the non-delegation doctrine to strike down legislation only twice in our history, both times in 1935, and both times dealing with the same statute. The statute in question was the National Industrial Recovery Act (NIRA), one of the first and, at the time, most important laws enacted by the Congress that swept into power with President Franklin Roosevelt and proceeded to enact much of President Roosevelt's "New Deal." *Panama Refining Co. v. Ryan*, 293 U.S. 388 (1935), dealt with Section 9(c) of the NIRA, which authorized the President to prohibit the interstate or foreign shipment of oil that was extracted in violation of any state law production quota or restriction. Examining that section, as well as the rest of the statute, an eight-justice majority could not find any standard governing the President's authority to restrict such oil shipments. Writing for the majority, Chief Justice Hughes wrote, "As to the transportation of oil production in excess of state permission, the Congress has declared no policy, has established no standard, has laid down no rule. There is no requirement, no definition of circumstances and conditions in which the transportation is to be allowed or prohibited." Only Justice Cardozo dissented.

In the second case from 1935, *A.L.A. Schechter Poultry Corp. v. United States*, 295 U.S. 495 (1935), the Court struck down another provision of NIRA, which authorized the President to promulgate "codes of fair competition." The statute authorized the President to promulgate a code for a given industry (for example, the wholesale poultry business in the New York City area), which would establish business and employment practices in that particular industry—for example, the wages they would pay and the business practices they would follow. (The point of such codes was to prevent ruinous competition for the much-reduced demand for goods and services during the Depression, on the theory that such competition would further depress wages and prices and contribute to a further downward spiral of economic activity.) The Court, again speaking through Chief Justice Hughes, found that the NIRA statute provided no meaningful guidance on what such codes should include or what goals they should aim to accomplish. This time the Court was unanimous.

After these two cases, which featured a statute that was perhaps historically unique in its generality and immensity of its grant of power to the President, the Court has never again struck down a statute on non-delegation grounds. This is remarkable because throughout the 1930s Congress continued to enact statutes that had extremely broad goals. For example, The Federal Communications Act authorized the Federal Communications Commission to regulate radio broadcasting to promote the "public interest, convenience, or necessity." Despite this broad goal, the Court upheld the statute against a non-delegation attack in *National Broadcasting Co. v. United States*, 319 U.S. 190 (1943). During this period the Court also upheld other statutes in which agencies were tasked with achieving similarly-broad goals. *E.g.*, *American Power & Light v. SEC*, 329 U.S. 90 (1946) (upholding a law authorizing the Securities and Exchange Commission to modify the structure of public utility holding companies so as to ensure that those structures were not "unduly or unnecessarily complicate[d]" and did not "unfairly or inequitably distribute voting power among security holders").

The Court's refusal to engage in stringent review of legislation for non-delegation violations probably stems from the difficulty of determining when legitimate congressional delegation of authority to agencies crosses the line into a non-delegation violation. Given that such congressional delegation is undoubtedly necessary given the complexity of modern regulatory problems, a more stringent application of the non-delegation doctrine would embroil the Court in subjective line-drawing between appropriate and over-broad delegations. It is also possible that the enactment of the Administrative Procedure Act (APA) in 1946, which instituted processes for public input into agency rulemaking, mitigated the most serious concerns about agency lawmaking being conducted without public participation.

Regardless of the reasons, the Court's retreat from serious non-delegation review might lead one to conclude that the non-delegation doctrine is a dead letter. (And, indeed, it is usually the wrong answer on an exam to suggest that a statute might be held to violate the non-delegation doctrine—but be careful about a question that involves a statute that closely resembles the NIRA!) But the non-delegation doctrine still has a role to play today. Most notably, it serves as an impetus to courts to impose narrower interpretations of statutes that, if read aggressively, could raise non-delegation concerns. For example, in *Industrial Union Department, AFL-CIO v. American Petroleum Institute*, 448 U.S. 607 (1980), a plurality of the Court gave a narrow interpretation to the power a statute granted to the Occupational Safety and Health Administration (OHSA) to prescribe workplace safety standards, on the theory that a broader interpretation would raise serious non-delegation concerns. Thus, even today, the non-delegation doctrine plays a role, though more as a canon of statutory interpretation than a constitutional limitation on Congress that courts feel competent to enforce fully.

In 2019, the Court decided a case in which it came the closest it has been since 1935 to resurrecting a more stringent version of the non-delegation doctrine. In *Gundy v. United States*, 139 S.Ct. 2116 (2019), a four-justice plurality followed the approach sketched out above to uphold the federal sex offender registration and notification statute. But the fifth justice, Justice Alito, expressed a willingness to join the three-justice dissent's call to fundamentally reconsider, and tighten up, the non-delegation doctrine. Since then, Justice Kavanaugh, who was not on the Court for *Gundy*, has expressed a similar willingness. It may be that a majority of the Court is now primed to strengthen the doctrine.

The short version: The non-delegation doctrine requires Congress to include an "intelligible principle" in statutes that grant quasi-legislative authority to agencies. The Court has found that legislation has failed this requirement only twice, both times in 1935. Today, the doctrine's main use is as a canon of statutory interpretation pushing courts toward more modest readings of statutes, rather than as a judicially-enforceable constitutional limit on legislation. However, the 2019 *Gundy* case signals that the Court today may be more interested in making non-delegation review more stringent.

CHAPTER 2

Congressional Power to Create Non-Article III Courts

In addition to delegating its own (legislative) power to agencies, Congress has also bestowed on agencies the power to adjudicate cases. This practice creates a potential conflict with another "vesting" clause, this one at the start of Article III, which vests "the judicial power of the United States . . . in one supreme Court, and in such inferior Courts as the Congress may from time to time ordain and establish." Article III, § 1, cl. 1. Such Article III courts are staffed by judges who are selected by the President and confirmed by the Senate, and enjoy life tenure with salary protections. But in addition to establishing such federal courts staffed by "Article III judges," Congress has also created adjudicative positions in agencies, staffed by so-called "administrative law judges" (ALJs), and sometimes called "agency courts" or "Article I courts" because they are created by Congress when using its Article I powers (for example, to regulate interstate commerce). Since Article III states that "the judicial power of the United States" is vested in Article III judges, questions have often arisen about the circumstances under which Congress can authorize non-Article III ALJs to possess some of "the judicial power of the United States."

The modern Court has followed an extremely unsteady path in answering this difficult question. In 1982, a plurality of the Court, in a case called *Northern Pipeline Construction Co. v. Marathon Pipe Line Co.*, 458 U.S. 50 (1982), insisted that, with very limited exceptions, Article I courts could only decide questions of what are called "public rights." (The concept of a "public right" is described below.) Four years later, in *Commodity Futures Trading Commission v. Schor*, 478 U.S. 833 (1986), the Court downgraded the importance of this issue, retaining it as a factor, but only one factor, in a multi-factor balancing test. Later cases have rested uneasily between these two approaches. Those cases are discussed below. But for now, let's focus on the idea of "public rights" and its converse, "private rights."

The public/private rights distinction was first expressly embraced by the Court in a nineteenth century case called *Murray's Lessee v. Hoboken Land Improvement Co.*, 59 U.S. 272 (1856). *Murray's Lessee* dealt with an attempt by the federal government to seize and sell the property of a customs inspector who was held to owe the federal government money from the customs duties he collected. The seizure and sale were accomplished without judicial order; nevertheless, the Court upheld that non-Article III-supervised process because a suit by the inspector against the government could only proceed if Congress waived its sovereign immunity. Because Congress could set the terms under which it could be sued (and could refuse to allow the United States to be sued at all), it was reasoned that Congress could take the lesser step and allow any adjudicative process to be performed by a non-Article III tribunal.

Since *Murray's Lessee*, it has come to be understood that the archetypical private right is one that is between two private parties (as opposed to one between a private party and the United States Government) and based on the common law (as opposed to federal statute). This simplified distinction between private and public rights hides a lot of ambiguity: however, because the claims at issue in both *Northern Pipeline* and *Schor* were between two private parties and based on the common law, the Court in both cases was able to evaluate the role of the public/private right distinction without recourse to more difficult definitional questions.

In *Schor*, Justice O'Connor's majority opinion observed that *Northern Pipeline*'s rigid insistence on Article I courts' ability to adjudicate only public rights commanded only a plurality, not a majority of the Court. She announced instead a multi-factor approach, which considered (1) the extent to which "the essential attributes" of Article III power remained with Article III courts, and conversely the extent to which those attributes were shared with Article I courts; (2) the private or public nature of the right; and (3) the reasons Congress had to create the agency court adjudication scheme. Applying the "essential attributes" factor, she noted that the scheme at issue in *Schor* itself involved an agency court that (a) did not have broad jurisdiction of the sort a federal district court enjoyed, (b) had powers more limited than those of an Article III court (for example, it could not convene jury trials, issue writs of *habeas corpus*, or enforce its own judgments), and (c) was subject to meaningful review by an Article III court on appeal. (In particular, she noted that the Article III court reviewed the agency court's legal conclusions *de novo*, that is, without any deference to the ALJ's legal interpretations.)

Moving to the second factor, Justice O'Connor conceded that the right at issue—a common-law contract claim that was brought by a commodities broker against his customer, in response to his customer's claim that the broker had violated federal commodities trading laws—had to be understood as a private right. But she argued that the nature of the right at issue as public or private mattered only because, as a matter of history, private rights were generally resolved by Article III courts. Conversely, there was less of a separation of powers problem when Congress gave an agency court the power to adjudicate a public right that Congress or the Executive could conclusively determine on its own, for example, by repealing the federal statute on which the right rested or, as noted in *Murray's Lessee*, by refusing to waive the government's sovereign immunity. Thus, while this factor mattered, she concluded that it only mattered as one factor in a balancing test.

Finally, Justice O'Connor noted that Congress had good reasons for setting up the agency adjudication scheme. The scheme in question involved adjudication of disputes over commodities transactions, which were regulated by a federal law about which the agency's ALJs could be expected to be very knowledgeable. To be sure, those ALJs also had jurisdiction over common law claims related to disputes over the federal statute—indeed, the claim that gave rise to the *Schor* case was the broker's common law claim that the customer has simply breached his commodities brokerage contract. But she observed that such jurisdiction paralleled supplemental (or "pendent") federal court jurisdiction, which was a long-accepted part of federal court jurisdiction. She noted that Congress had intended for such statutory claims to be resolved through an expeditious and procedurally-streamlined process, which could only be made effective if the ALJ also had jurisdiction over common-law counterclaims that related to the subject-matter of the statutory claim. She also noted that Congress did not attempt to exert any control over the adjudication scheme, that the agency in question was perceived to be "relatively immune from political pressures," that the agency's jurisdiction was in addition to, rather than a replacement for, federal court jurisdiction, and finally, that Congress did not set up the Article I court scheme in order to punish Article III courts for ruling in certain ways.

Nevertheless, in the years after *Schor* the Court sometimes focused more intensively on the nature of the right as determining the constitutionality of an agency adjudication scheme. In *Granfinanciera, S.A. v. Nordberg*, 492 U.S. 33 (1989), Justice Brennan, who wrote the plurality in *Northern Pipeline*, again tried to focus the Court's doctrine on the public/private rights issue. *Granfinanciera* was not a case about the constitutionality of an Article I adjudication scheme *per se*; instead, it involved a question of when a party enjoyed the Seventh Amendment right to a jury trial in a civil case. But he decided that both questions should be answered the same way—by recourse to the public/private rights distinction.

However, in a way that bedevils lawyers and students, Justice Brennan also *redefined* "public" rights. Quoting an earlier, pre-*Schor*, case, he wrote: "The crucial question, in cases not involving the Federal Government, is whether 'Congress, acting for a valid legislative purpose pursuant to its constitutional powers under Article I, [has] create[d] a seemingly "private" right that is so closely integrated into a public regulatory scheme as to be a matter appropriate for agency resolution with limited involvement by the Article III judiciary.' "

More recent cases have continued to vacillate between *Schor*'s multi-factor test and *Granfinanciera*'s reliance on the public/private rights distinction, with "public rights" defined more broadly than before. This ambivalence is reflected in two bankruptcy cases. In *Stern v. Marshall*, 564 U.S. 462 (2011), the Court insisted that a bankruptcy court (an Article I court) could only adjudicate public rights (again, using the broader definition of "public right"). By contrast, in *Wellness Int'l Network, Ltd v. Sharif*, 575 U.S. 665 (2015), the Court, describing *Schor* as "foundational," applied that case's balancing test. Indeed, it did not even discuss the nature of the right at issue as public or private.

The take-away from all this is, as you can imagine, complicated. *Schor* does seem to be the foundational case on point, as recently reinforced by *Wellness International*. At the very least, its more accepting attitude toward agency courts reappears even in cases that apply a rigid public/private right distinction in deciding such questions. Indeed, even in *Stern*, the Court described "public rights" in the broad terms described in *Granfinanciera*, and described the common-law counterclaim in *Schor* as one whose adjudication by the agency court was "essential" to the agency court's resolution of the statutory claim everyone agreed the ALJ could adjudicate. Thus, regardless of which approach a court takes, many claims—including those that seem at first glance to implicate private rights—appear to be amenable to adjudication by a non-Article III court. At most, the only claims that might be immune to such adjudication are those based on rights that appear to be private, and that are not "closely integrated into a public regulatory scheme."

The short version: Congress retains significant authority to grant agencies adjudicative power that would otherwise be wielded by Article III courts. While the Court has not been completely consistent, such grants of adjudicative power will generally be scrutinized based on a set of factors, including: whether the agency adjudicator lacks the powers and jurisdiction of an Article III court, whether an Article III court retains meaningful review authority over the agency court's decisions, whether the agency court is authorized to decide cases only of "public rights," and whether Congress authorized the agency adjudication for appropriate reasons.

CHAPTER 3

Presidential Control over Agency Officers

The first two chapters dealt with congressional attempts to give agencies powers normally wielded by, respectively, Congress itself and Article III courts. This leaves the Executive branch itself. In the context of the Executive branch, the relevant question is *not* whether Congress can give agencies powers normally wielded by the Executive branch. After all, we normally think about agencies as being part of the Executive branch. Instead, the question this chapter takes up involves issues of presidential control—in particular, the extent to which the President has the constitutional authority to appoint, control, and remove high-ranking administrative officials.

The appointments issue turns explicitly on constitutional text— the Appointments Clause of Article II, § 2, clause 2. That clause reads, in relevant part:

> "He [the President] . . . shall nominate, and by and with the Advice and Consent of the senate, shall appoint Ambassadors, other public Ministers and Consuls, Judges of the supreme Court, and all other Officers of the United

States . . .: but the Congress may by Law vest the Appointment of such inferior Officers, as they think proper, in the President alone, in the Courts of Law or in the Heads of Departments."

Before considering the principal/inferior officer distinction, note that there is another class of federal officials not mentioned in Article II: "employees." When one thinks of a federal government "employee," one likely thinks of persons such as letter carriers or clerks in government offices. However, in *Lucia v. SEC*, 138 S.Ct. 2044 (2018), the Court considered a claim that ALJs within the SEC were mere employees. The Court rejected that argument, concluding that they were officers. In doing so, it relied heavily on precedent (the *Freytag* case cited two paragraphs below) that had found trial judges in the (Article I) Tax Court to be officers. The *Lucia* Court concluded that the SEC's ALJs had similar authority to those tax court judges, and thus were similarly "officers," not mere "employees." (The Court did not have to decide whether they were "principal" or "inferior" officers.)

Turn now to the two categories of officers. As the Appointments Clause suggests, a crucial question for the President's appointment power is whether the officer in question is an "Officer of the United States" (sometimes called a "principal officer"), in which case the appointment power rests with the President, or an "inferior officer," in which case Congress can place the appointment power in several places, including but not limited to the President.

The Court has decided a series of cases that attempt to clarify the principal/inferior officer distinction. Taken together, these cases (*Morrison v. Olson*, 487 U.S. 654 (1988); *Freytag v. Com'r of Internal Revenue*, 501 U.S. 868 (1991); *Edmond v. United States*, 520 U.S. 651 (1997); *Free Enterprise Fund v. Public Company Accounting and Oversight Board*, 561 U.S. 477 (2010); and *United*

States v. Arthrex, Inc., 141 S.Ct. 1970 (2021)) stand for the proposition that the principal/inferior distinction can be drawn by referring to concepts such as the degree to which the officer's work was subject to supervision and control by a higher-ranking officer, and the character of the limitations on the officer's powers. The important point here is that there is not a bright-line distinction between the two types of officers. Thus, decisions about a particular officer's status will be heavily fact-dependent.

In comparison to the appointment power, the question of the President's control and removal power is based less on constitutional text; instead, the Court's decisions have rested more on underlying structural principles, in particular, Article II's statement that "the executive power" is vested in the President. In *Myers v. United States*, 272 U.S. 52 (1926), the Court decided that Congress unconstitutionally intruded on that power when it restricted the President's ability to fire postmasters. The Court's opinion, written by Chief Justice (and former president) William Howard Taft, amounted to a strong endorsement of presidential authority to remove high-ranking agency officials. Nine years later, in *Humphrey's Executor v. United States*, 295 U.S. 602 (1935), the Court cut back on that authority. *Humphrey's Executor* upheld a decision by Congress to limit the President's power to fire commissioners of the Federal Trade Commission (FTC). The Court concluded that because the FTC engaged in quasi-legislative and quasi-judicial work, it did not violate the president's powers to limit his control over the tenure of FTC commissioners, by fixing a set term of office for those commissioners and limiting the circumstances under which a commissioner could be removed before the end of that term.

The law changed in *Morrison v. Olson*, discussed earlier in this chapter. In addition to interpreting the Appointments Clause (noted earlier in this chapter), that case also considered presidential removal power. *Morrison* dealt with a law establishing a process for the appointment and removal of "special prosecutors" designed to allow investigation into possible illegal acts by White House officials. Among other things, that law limited the President's power to fire the special prosecutor to situations where there was "good cause" to fire her.

The *Morrison* Court held that this limitation did not unconstitutionally intrude on presidential power. Chief Justice Rehnquist, writing for eight justices, acknowledged that *Humphrey's Executor* might have suggested the opposite result— after all, the official in question in *Morrison* was a prosecutor, that is, someone who acted not in a quasi-legislative or quasi-judicial capacity, but someone whose main job was to enforce the laws. This would suggest that, under *Humphrey's Executor*, the President retained Article II authority to fire that person at will. But *Morrison* rejected *Humphrey's Executor*'s approach. Instead, it wrote that the relevant test was "whether the removal restrictions are of such a nature that they impede the President's ability to perform his constitutional duty." He conceded that, in answering that question, the nature of the functions the official performed was not irrelevant. However, it was also not dispositive. In *Morrison*, the Court concluded that the power the President retained to fire the prosecutor for "good cause," when combined with the fact that the prosecutor was an inferior rather than a principal officer, meant that the law did not unconstitutionally restrict the President's power.

Humphrey's Executor and *Morrison* can be thought of as strong endorsements of congressional authority to immunize administrative officials from presidential removal-at-will power. *Humphrey's Executor* made it clear that so-called "independent agencies" (*e.g.*, the Federal Communications Commission and the Federal Reserve Board) can be headed by officers that are not subject to removal at will by the President. *Morrison*, by validating Congress's decision to immunize even an officer who performed a core law-enforcing function, arguably gave even more power to Congress to immunize important agency officials.

The Court cut back somewhat on this restrictive approach to presidential control in *Free Enterprise Fund v. Public Company Accounting Oversight Board*, 561 U.S. 477 (2010). *Free Enterprise Fund* considered the constitutionality of the "good cause" restriction to removal of members of the Public Company Accounting Oversight Board (PCAOB). Members of the PCAOB were appointed for a term of years by commissioners of the Securities and Exchange Commission (SEC), and were removable by those commissioners before that term was up only for good cause. Importantly, the Court decided the case on the assumption that SEC members themselves were similarly appointed for a term of years by the President, and were similarly removable before that term only for good cause. Thus, members of the PCAOB were doubly-insulated from presidential removal-at-will.

According to a five-justice majority, that double insulation made the case different from *Morrison* in a way that led to a different constitutional result. Chief Justice Roberts concluded that this double insulation simply took away too much authority, and thus accountability, from the President, by making it too difficult for the President to effectively oversee the work of the PCAOB, if necessary by firing its members.

Free Enterprise Fund dealt only with members of the PCAOB. But Justice Breyer, the author of the dissent in that case, cautioned that its impact might be much broader. He noted, for example, that ALJs are also doubly insulated from presidential removal at-will: they are removable only for good cause, and the procedures for such removal are set by a federal agency whose leaders, just like commissioners of the SEC, are themselves removable by the

President only for good cause. *Free Enterprise Fund* thus opens questions about such double-insulation situations throughout the federal bureaucracy.

Ten years after *Free Enterprise Fund*, in *Seila Law LLC v. Consumer Financial Protection Bureau*, 140 S.Ct. 2183 (2020), the Court cut back even more on *Morrison* and *Humphrey's Executor*. *Seila Law* dealt with a for-cause removal restriction on an agency headed by a single-member principal officer. Thus, the Court explained, the case was not controlled by *Morrison*, which involved an inferior officer, or by *Humphrey's Executor*, which involved a multi-member-headed agency (the Federal Trade Commission).

The Court struck down the good-cause limitation. Importantly, it described *Morrison* and *Humphrey's Executor* as exceptions to the general rule, which it identified as *Myers'* broad presidential control authority. *Seila Law* seems to make it unlikely that further "exceptions" will be in the offing. Indeed, it sets up the Court, if it wishes, to overrule those two existing exceptions.

The short version: Article II requires that the President be able to appoint principal officers, but Congress may vest the appointment of "inferior officers" in either the President, the courts, or the "Heads of Departments." The line between principal and inferior officers is not a clear one, but if an officer is subject to control by another officer then the Court will often consider the officer in question to be "inferior." The President's Article II-based authority to fire officers at will turns on whether divesting him of that power would impair his ability to carry out his Article II duties to execute the laws, although in recent years the Court has understood the President's removal power more broadly than before.

CHAPTER 4

Congressional Retention of Delegated Power: The Legislative Veto and the Congressional Review Act

Chapter 1 concluded that the non-delegation doctrine does not stand as a powerful barrier to Congress delegating away important policy decisions to agencies. One might think, therefore, that Congress would be able to retain a measure of control over agencies when it delegates such power.

At a basic level, Congress does, of course, retain such power, because it can always repeal the statute that granted the agency that power in the first place. However, this is often not an optimal way for Congress to exert such control. Repealing a statute is a very blunt instrument for retaining control, especially if the underlying regulatory problem that motivated the original delegation remains. For example, repealing the Clean Air Act is one way of controlling how the Environmental Protection Agency (EPA) administers that statute, but the problem of air pollution will remain, and will presumably require some legislative response (and thus, quite likely some new delegation of power to the EPA).

More specifically, Congress can overturn a particular regulation by enacting a statute explicitly rejecting it. This happens rarely, because, at least with regulations promulgated by an executive (as opposed to an independent) agency, presumably the President and the President's appointee as the agency head are sufficiently supportive of such regulations that a congressional repeal attempt would trigger a hard-to-override presidential veto. Nevertheless, this option remains open, especially with regard to regulations promulgated while one president is in office and which are subject to repeal when another president of a different party takes control. The Congressional Review Act (CRA), discussed below, provides a special procedure for statutory overrides of agency actions.

One option Congress had frequently employed before 1983 was to insert into many organic statutes a so-called "legislative veto." As the name implies, a "legislative veto" is a decision by Congress to disapprove, or "veto," an agency action. But a legislative veto is different from a standard statutory rejection of an agency action because it doesn't go through all the requirements the Constitution sets forth in Article I, Section 7 to enact a bill into law. Thus, for example, a legislative veto could provide that such a rejection of an agency action would become effective upon its approval by both houses of Congress, without presentment to the President. Indeed, it could also provide that such a rejection would become effective upon only one house approving it.

Such a one-house veto was at issue in *Immigration and Naturalization Service v. Chadha*, 462 U.S. 919 (1983). *Chadha* dealt with authority Congress had granted to the Attorney General under the Immigration and Nationality Act (INA) to suspend the deportation of any alien who would otherwise be subject to deportation. In addition to granting that power to the Attorney

General, the INA also provided that either house of Congress could disapprove of such a suspension decision. When the Attorney General decided to suspend the deportation of an alien named Chadha (and thus to allow him to remain in the United States), the House of Representatives voted to veto that suspension.

The Court struck down the legislative veto in that case and, by extension, all legislative vetoes. Speaking for seven Justices, Chief Justice Burger laid out Article I's lawmaking process, noted the exceptions to that process (for example, the requirement that 2/3 of the Senate concur in order for a treaty to become ratified and binding law), and concluded that the veto of the Attorney General's decision to suspend Chadha's deportation constituted lawmaking (because it changed Mr. Chadha's legal rights). Given this train of logic, he concluded that legislative vetoes—whether one-house, as in *Chadha* itself, or two-house—violated the Constitution's process for lawmaking.

Justice Powell agreed with the result, but based his vote on his conclusion that Congress had taken upon itself the role of adjudicator, by passing judgment on a particular person's case. Justice White dissented, arguing that the underlying principles of bicameralism (approval by both houses) and presentment (the requirement that any bill be presented to the President for signature or formal veto) were satisfied in this case. Justice White stressed the importance of allowing Congress to adopt innovative ways of controlling administrative agency action, given its practice (seemingly approved by the Court) of delegating broad swaths of its power to agencies.

Despite these separate opinions, the clear result of *Chadha* is that legislative vetoes are unconstitutional. Of course, Congress always retains the option of attempting to enact a full-blown statute rejecting a particular agency action. But, again, that option requires agreement from both houses and, most importantly, the concurrence of the President, or a super-majority to override his veto. The legislative veto offered a way of avoiding those difficulties—but one that the Court ultimately found unconstitutional.

One way Congress has attempted to make it easier to control agency action is through the Congressional Review Act (CRA), noted above. Essentially, the CRA creates a streamlined procedural path for the enactment of a statute disapproving of an agency action. The CRA was enacted in 1996, and before 2017 was used very sparingly. In 2017 Congress used it several times to repeal regulations promulgated during the Obama Administration. An important aspect of the CRA is its provision that a regulation rescinded via a CRA disapproval resolution could not be re-promulgated later by an agency unless Congress specifically authorized that re-promulgation. Thus, the CRA attempts to avoid the problem of an agency simply waiting for a new Congress and then re-promulgating the regulation that the earlier Congress had disapproved.

Beyond formally rescinding regulations, Congress retains other important mechanisms for controlling agencies. Congress—and in particular, the relevant committees that have jurisdiction over a given agency—still has to approve the agency's budget requests. In addition, the Senate has the power to approve or reject the President's nominees for the top leadership positions in each agency. Finally, the relevant committees engage in ongoing communication with agency staff, and can call agency personnel to testify if necessary. Many of these tools are blunt, and not well-suited to the sort of micro-managing that the legislative veto allowed. Others can be more carefully fine-tuned, but, as informal controls, their efficacy depends on the facts of the particular situation. Still, it remains the case that Congress retains many formal and informal means for influencing agency action short of a formal statute disapproving a particular regulation.

The short version: If Congress wishes to overrule an agency action it may only do so via a full-blown statute, because legislative vetoes have been declared unconstitutional. The Congressional Review Act, however, provides a procedurally-streamlined way for Congress to enact such statutes. In addition, Congress retains significant informal influence over agencies, through matters such as budgeting and Senate confirmation of key agency personnel.

* * * * *

THE TAKEAWAY

What are the main issues this Part addresses?

- **Congress's ability to give agencies power to act in quasi-legislative ways.**

  The non-delegation doctrine requires that Congress provide agencies with "an intelligible principle" in the statutes it enacts. This is a very lenient requirement; today, the doctrine acts less as a judicially-imposed limit on Congress and more as canon of statutory interpretation that favors narrow readings of otherwise broad grants of power to agencies.

- **Congress's ability to give agencies the power to adjudicate.**

  While the Court has not been completely consistent, as a general matter the Court seems to give Congress broad power to grant agencies adjudicative power that would otherwise vest in Article III courts. Under the *Schor* test such agency courts should not possess all the normal powers of an Article III court, should be subject to meaningful Article III court review, should be limited, at least in some cases, in their ability to adjudicate private rights (however such rights are defined), and should be created by Congress for appropriate reasons.

- **The President's constitutional authority to appoint key administrators.**

  Article II gives the President the right to name principal officers of the United States; however, Congress may place the appointment of an "inferior" officer in either the President, the Article III courts, or the "Heads of Departments." Generally speaking, an inferior officer is one that is subject to the control of a principal officer.

- **The President's constitutional authority to remove key administrators.**

  As long as the limitation does not "impede" the President's ability to perform his Article II duties, Congress may limit the President's ability to remove an inferior officer by requiring that such firing be only for "good cause." In recent years, the Court has increased presidential removal authority.

- **Congressional control over how agencies use their delegated power.**

  Congress may not use a legislative veto to reverse agency actions with which it disagrees. However, the Congressional Review Act provides a streamlined process for Congress to enact legislation reversing such actions. In addition, Congress has many informal mechanisms of influence over agencies, such as control over budgets and Senate confirmation of senior agency staff.

The Rulemaking Process

Rulemaking is the bread-and-butter of administrative law. Regulations promulgated by federal administrative agencies touch every aspect of Americans' lives. It is probably a fair statement that, with the exception of criminal law, the legal duties Americans owe and legal rights Americans have come more directly from regulations than from statutes. For these reasons, it is important to understand the process by which such regulations are developed and ultimately promulgated. Chapter 5 provides an introduction to rulemaking. Chapter 6 sets forth the processes agencies are required to use when they engage in rulemaking. Chapter 7 explains the situations in which agencies are exempt from those processes. Chapter 8 considers issues of bias and prejudgment in rulemaking. Chapter 9 sets forth executive branch initiatives designed to increase presidential control over rulemaking.

CHAPTER 5

An Introduction to Rulemaking

This chapter sets forth some of the basics about rulemaking, before later chapters explain that process in more detail. Most of this chapter considers how rulemaking is different from adjudication, the other main vehicle by which agencies can act. It ends by considering the question of agencies' authority to engage in rulemaking.

A. The Rulemaking/Adjudication Distinction

Before examining the rulemaking process, it is important to understand the distinction between rulemaking and adjudication, the other main vehicle by which agencies exercise coercive power over individuals. Intuitively, one can think of rulemaking as akin to legislating, while agency adjudication is akin to judicial adjudication. This parallel isn't perfect, but it provides a rough guidepost.

The Administrative Procedure Act (APA) defines the products of both of these processes. The APA defines a "rule" (the end product of a rulemaking) to include "the whole or a part of an agency statement of general or particular applicability and future effect designed to implement, interpret, or prescribe law or policy." 5 U.S.C. § 551(4). It defines "order" (the end product of an adjudication) as "the whole or a part of a final disposition, whether affirmative, negative, injunctive, or declaratory in form, of an agency in a matter other than rule making." 5 U.S.C. § 551(6). The definition of "rule" largely tracks our intuitive understandings of legislation (a generally applicable rule of conduct with mainly prospective application), with the important difference that an administrative "rule" can in fact have not "general," but "particular" applicability. For example, when an agency sets the rates a particular company can charge, that action is considered a rulemaking, even though it is focused on that particular company.

Despite this relatively clear definition, significant ambiguities sometimes make it difficult to know whether an agency has in fact promulgated a rule as opposed to an order. One of the most famous examples of this ambiguity is the action of the National Labor Relations Board (NLRB) challenged in *NLRB v. Wyman-Gordon Co.*, 394 U.S. 759 (1969). In *Wyman-Gordon*, the NLRB ordered a company to disclose to a labor union a list of its employees' names and addresses. (As you can imagine, such a list would be very helpful to the union's attempts to communicate with the workers it is trying to unionize.) In support of that order, the agency cited one of its earlier decisions, a case called *Excelsior Underwear*, which announced a new rule requiring such disclosures. However, the company in *Wyman-Gordon* argued that the *Excelsior* decision was invalid, and thus could not serve as support for the order against it.

The company's argument, which a majority of a fractured Court accepted in the course of several opinions, was that the *Excelsior* decision, which the agency described as an adjudication, was in fact a rulemaking that failed to follow the APA's rulemaking procedures. The problem, according to the Court, was that the agency did not apply the *Excelsior* decision to the parties in that particular case, but rather, given its novelty, imposed the disclosure rule only prospectively. According to the Court, this transformed the *Excelsior* proceeding from an adjudication to a rulemaking. But because the agency in the *Excelsior* case only invited certain parties to participate in the briefing and oral argument, the agency violated the rulemaking procedures of the APA, which allow any interested person to participate.

The facts of *Wyman-Gordon* are tangled, but the underlying lesson is straightforward: the line between adjudication and rulemaking is not as clearly demarcated as our initial intuition might suggest. The rest of this *Guide* will assume that we know what we're talking about when we describe an agency action as a rulemaking or an adjudication. But it's important to realize that that assumption may not always be warranted—or at least that you need to keep that ambiguity in the back of your mind.

B. The Implications of the Rulemaking/ Adjudication Distinction

Whether an agency action is considered a rulemaking or an adjudication has important implications for the process the agency is required to follow. Beyond defining the two concepts (as noted in the previous section), the APA also imposes different procedural requirements for the two, as noted in Chapter 6 (rulemaking) and Chapters 12 and 13 (adjudication). The distinction also has constitutional dimensions. The Due Process Clauses of the Fifth Amendment (applicable to the federal government) and the Fourteenth Amendment (applicable to the states) mandate a particular level of procedure when government impairs a person's interest in "life, liberty, or property." But those clauses apply only when the government is acting in a way that can be labelled as adjudicative.

The distinction between what the Due Process Clauses require in cases of rulemaking and adjudication was set forth in a pair of important cases from the early twentieth century. In *Londoner v. Denver*, 210 U.S. 373 (1908), the Court held that due process required at least an informal oral hearing before the government imposed an assessment on an individual property owner to recover the cost of paving a road that abutted his property. Seven years later, in *Bi-Metallic Investment Co. v. State Board of Equalization*, 239 U.S. 441 (1915), the Court distinguished *Londoner*, and held that no hearing was required when a decision was made to revalue upward, for property tax assessment purposes, every property in a city. Justice Holmes, writing in *Bi-Metallic*, distinguished *Londoner* on the ground that, in that earlier case, "[a] relatively small number of persons was concerned, who were exceptionally affected, in each case upon individual grounds." The factors he mentions—the generality or specificity of the effect, and the question whether the persons in question are affected on grounds unique to them or simply as members of a class—track our intuitions about the distinction between legislation and adjudication, and reinforce the idea that the Due Process Clauses apply only in adjudications.

C. Agency Discretion to Choose Between Rulemaking and Adjudication

Once we have a basic sense of the difference between rulemaking and adjudication, the next question concerns the leeway agencies enjoy to proceed by one or the other of these vehicles. To return to our legislation/adjudication analogy, rulemaking is usually (1) generally applicable and (2) prospective, while adjudication is usually (1) applicable only to one party and (2) retrospective. To over-simplify, consider a situation where the agency becomes responsible for implementing a newly-enacted statute. It can do so either by promulgating regulations and only after that point bringing enforcement actions that allege a violation of the statute and/or those regulations, or it can move directly to bringing enforcement actions alleging violations only of the statute itself.

In case law the claim is usually that the agency used case-by-case adjudication when it should have been required to proceed by rulemaking. This is an understandable position. Because of its prospectivity and general applicability, as a general policy matter rulemaking is often seen as the preferred approach. Rulemaking affects all similarly-situated persons equally, because a rule on a given issue applies to everyone who engages in that conduct. By contrast, case-by-case adjudications, by definition, single out particular parties as defendants, thus raising the risk or at least the perception of unfairness or selective prosecution. In addition, the prospectivity of rulemaking—that is, the fact that the rules of conduct it imposes apply only going forward in the future, not to conduct that has already occurred—lessens the possibility of unfair surprise that might accompany a retrospective adjudication (especially one that imposes fines or other serious sanctions for violations).

Despite these generally-conceded advantages to rulemaking, there are good reasons why an agency might choose to proceed via case-by-case adjudication. In an important case, *SEC v. Chenery Corp.*, 332 U.S. 194 (1947), the Court set forth several reasons an agency might legitimately choose to proceed via adjudication rather than rulemaking. First, an agency might not be able to foresee problems that require a quick resolution, rather than a resolution that would have to await the (sometimes lengthy) process of crafting and promulgating a rule. Second, the agency might not have the experience with a particular issue that would justify it promulgating a hard and fast rule before it was sure what the proper regulatory response should be. Finally, *Chenery* noted that some problems may be so fact- or context-specific that they are incapable of encapsulation in a generally-worded rule. For these reasons, it concluded that the choice between proceeding by rulemaking or adjudication had to remain within the agency's discretion.

Chenery did, however, acknowledge limitations on this discretion. First, it observed (without much elaboration) that such discretion might be abused. Second, it noted that a decision to proceed by adjudication might lead to the imposition of retroactive liability that would be extremely unfair. It cautioned, though, that such unfairness would have to be balanced against "the mischief of producing a result which is contrary to a statutory design or to legal and equitable principles." If that "mischief" outweighed the unfairness to the regulated party of imposing retroactive liability, then, it concluded, the law did not condemn such liability.

Courts since *Chenery* have generally given agencies extremely broad leeway to choose between rulemaking and adjudication. For example, in *NLRB v. Bell Aerospace*, 416 U.S. 267 (1974), the Court upheld the agency's decision to proceed case-by-case when determining that a particular group of employees were not managers, and thus were eligible for unionization. The Court explained that because employees' duties varied so greatly across the economy, any general rule would be unable to capture all the factors that would be relevant in a given case. One notable exception to this general rule of deference to the agency is a circuit court case, *Ford Motor Co. v. Federal Trade Commission*, 673 F.2d 1008 (9th Cir. 1981). In that case, the agency began enforcement actions (that is, adjudications) against car dealers and manufacturers' finance subsidiaries, to challenge how dealers estimated the value of cars they repossess for purposes of determining how much money the former owner would be due. The agency clearly intended the result of those adjudications to apply to the entire industry; indeed, the agency had prepared a statement to be sent to all dealers upon the conclusion of the cases, advising them of the decisions. The appellate panel (over one dissent) concluded that these facts established the generally applicable nature of the adjudicative result, which in turn meant that the decision should have been rendered via a rulemaking.

Ford Motor, however, has not generally been followed. Today, in most cases the agency has extremely broad discretion to choose either rulemaking or adjudication, subject to what seems to be marginal limitations of the sort acknowledged in *Chenery*.

D. Agency Authority to Engage in Rulemaking

One final preliminary point about rulemaking, before we delve into the procedures agencies must use when promulgating a rule: agencies need authority to engage in rulemaking. This authority does not come from the APA itself. Rather, the agency's organic statute must provide that rulemaking authority. Thus, for example, the Clean Air Act authorizes the Environmental Protection Agency to promulgate regulations to implement that statute.

This hurdle—the requirement that agencies possess statutory authority to promulgate regulations—is generally not a difficult one to surmount. In light of the many advantages courts perceive from rulemaking, they are generally willing to find such authority even in statutes that are not explicit about it.

The short version: The rulemaking/adjudication distinction is fundamental to administrative law. Due process rights apply only to adjudication. While generally agency adjudication is analogous to judicial action and rulemaking to legislation, this common-sense distinction breaks down at the margins. As a general matter, agencies have a great deal of discretion to choose to act via either rulemaking or adjudication.

CHAPTER 6

Formal and Informal Rulemaking

As a general matter, the APA sets forth the process agencies must follow when they engage in rulemaking. That statute distinguishes between formal and informal processes. This chapter will discuss those two different processes, and then the agency's discretion to choose between them.

Before we move to that discussion, however, one important point needs to be made about the first sentence of this chapter, above: *"As a general matter, the APA sets forth the process agencies must follow when they engage in rulemaking."* The first four words are italicized because it cannot be too often repeated that the APA is a default statute. Congress, when enacting the organic statute that authorizes an agency to take certain actions, can always prescribe the process it wants that particular agency to follow when implementing that particular statute. Often, Congress does not provide such specific procedures. In that case, the APA's procedures apply. But when considering what process an agency has to follow, you always need to make sure that the organic statute doesn't supersede the APA by prescribing processes that apply to that particular regulatory program.

A. Rulemaking Procedures Applicable to Both Formal and Informal Rulemaking

The APA's rulemaking procedures—both formal and informal—are grounded in Section 553 (5 U.S.C. § 553). Subsection (a) sets forth some types of rules that are completely exempt from those required procedures. (Chapter 7 covers the exemptions to the rulemaking process.) Subsection (b) requires that agencies provide notice—either "general" notice, or, in the case of rules that are more particularly targeted (for example, rulemakings to set allowable rates), notice to those particular persons.

Subsection (c) spells out the actual participation rights persons have in a rulemaking. This is where formal and informal rulemaking diverge. These divergent procedures are spelled out in the next two sections. Subsection (d) requires that the required publication or service of a rule be made at least 30 days before the rule's effective date. Subsection (e) gives all persons a right to petition the agency to issue, amend, or repeal a rule.

In sum, then, these requirements (leaving aside subsection (c)) require notice, publication or other notification before the rule's effective date, and the right to request the agency to consider promulgating a rule or its amendment or repeal.

B. Formal Rulemaking Hearings

The difference between formal and informal rulemaking processes is in the type of hearing that agencies must provide. As noted in the next section, agencies that are able to take advantage of informal rulemaking must simply give interested parties a chance to submit written comments, and must provide a "concise and general statement" of the "basis and purpose" of the rule that the agency ultimately promulgates. While this process does not necessarily guarantee a quick and easy rulemaking, the written nature of the participation process is, at least in theory, straightforward and simple.

By contrast, agencies engaging in formal rulemaking must comply with the more elaborate requirements of Sections 556 and 557 of the APA. Those APA sections impose a variety of requirements on agencies. Speaking broadly, they require procedures that are at least somewhat akin to a judicial trial, although you should be careful not to assume that formal agency proceedings are precisely analogous to judicial trials.

Section 556 specifies that either an ALJ or the agency head (or one or more of the heads in the case of a multi-member agency) shall preside "at the taking of evidence." Section 556(b). The presiding person or persons has/have the power essentially to run the hearing, for example by having depositions taken and issuing subpoenas. Section 556(c). (You should read Section 556(c) to see all the conduct that the presiding officer controls, and thus all the conduct that is assumed to be part of a formal agency proceeding.) Section 556(d) states that "the proponent of a rule or order" (for example, the agency when it proposes a rule in a formal rulemaking) has the burden of proof. Importantly, that same section states that "Any oral or documentary evidence may be received, but the agency as a matter of policy shall provide for the exclusion of irrelevant, immaterial, or unduly repetitious evidence." It also states that "A party is entitled to present his case or defense by oral or documentary evidence, to submit rebuttal evidence, and to conduct such cross-examination as may be required for a full and true disclosure of the facts." It's also important to note that this same subsection (556(d)) states, in part, that "In rule making . . . an agency may, when a party will not be prejudiced thereby, adopt procedures for the submission of all or part of the evidence in written form." Thus, while Section 556 contemplates a formalized process akin to a judicial trial, at times it bends in the direction of allowing the presiding agency official(s) to streamline that process.

Section 556(e) concludes this section by providing that "The transcript of testimony and exhibits, together with all papers and requests filed in the proceeding, constitutes the exclusive record for decision." This subsection establishes that decisions made after formal proceedings must rest solely on the record created during that proceeding. In other words, the decision-maker cannot justify his decision based on private information not made part of that public proceeding and thus not placed on the public record.

Section 557 adds several requirements to formal agency proceedings. For current purposes, the most relevant of these requirements are found in Section 557(c). That subsection provides that:

> "Before a recommended, initial, or tentative decision, or a decision on agency review of the decision of subordinate employees, the parties are entitled to a reasonable opportunity to submit for the consideration of the employees participating in the decisions—
>
> (1) proposed findings and conclusions; or
>
> (2) exceptions to the decisions or recommended decisions of subordinate employees or to tentative agency decisions; and
>
> (3) supporting reasons for the exceptions or proposed findings or conclusions."

This provision reinforces the sense from Section 556 that decisions under Section 557 must rest on relatively formalized fact findings and legal conclusions. Subsection (c)(3) also suggests that the agency's decision must be supported by reasons, and presumably must account for the reasons offered for findings or conclusions the agency rejected.

Section 557(d) restricts *ex parte* contacts between agency personnel and interested persons outside the agency. This provision is discussed later, in Chapter 8.

To repeat, the APA allows agencies to waive or streamline many of these procedural formalities when appropriate. Nevertheless, judges and scholars refer to these procedures as "trial-type" procedures. And with good reason. As compared with informal rulemaking procedures, described in the next section of this chapter, or informal adjudications, governed almost exclusively by the Due Process Clause, as described in Chapter 13, these proceedings are indeed quite formal.

C. Informal Rulemaking Procedures

The main distinction between formal and informal rulemaking is that the latter generally contemplates purely written participation by interested parties. To be sure, Section 553(c), the source for informal rulemaking requirements, states that "the agency shall give interested persons an opportunity to participate in the rule making through submission of written data, views, or arguments *with or without opportunity for oral presentation.*" (emphasis added). However, informal rulemaking is generally understood to embrace a default rule of written-only participation, with no obligation on the agency's part to provide for an oral hearing.

1. The Transformation of Notice and Comment Rulemaking

The relatively skeletal requirements of subsections (b), (d), and (e) of Section 553, when combined with the adequacy of a purely written hearing, would seem to suggest that informal rulemaking—also called "notice and comment" rulemaking because of its main components—is relatively quick and simple for agencies to perform. However, in the 1970s lower courts began interpreting those procedures in more expansive ways, with the result that today informal notice-and-comment rulemaking process can in fact be quite elaborate.

This expansion of notice-and-comment requirements impacted several parts of the process. First, courts began requiring a much more robust statement of the description of the proposed rule that had to be included in the notice. Recall that Section 553(b) states that that notice should include, among other things, "either the terms or substance of the proposed rule or a description of the subjects and issues involved." In cases such as *United States v. Nova Scotia Food Products Corp.*, 568 F.2d 240 (2d Cir. 1977), courts began requiring agencies to provide much of the scientific and technical background and justification for the proposed rule. Interestingly, this expansion was often justified less as a matter of ensuring compliance with subsection (b)'s notice requirement and more as an interpretation of subsection (c)'s provision of a right to comment. The theory is that the right to comment doesn't mean much if persons interested in commenting literally do not know what to say in their comments, because they had no access to the data or the reasoning underlying the agency's proposed rule.

Second, courts began insisting that the agency's *final* statement of the rule contain much more by way of justification and, in particular, responses to the comments received. Recall that Section 553(c) requires merely that the agency provide a "concise general statement" of the final rule's "basis and purpose." Nevertheless, again, courts reasoned that the right to comment would be of little value if commenters (and reviewing courts) did not know how the agency had responded to comments it received—

indeed, whether the agency had considered the comments at all. These courts also explained that a more detailed statement of the agency's responses to the comments it received was necessary in order for courts to determine, not just compliance with the notice-and-comment *procedures*, but also compliance with the *substantive* requirement that agency action not be "arbitrary and capricious." (The "arbitrary and capricious" standard is discussed later, in Chapter 23.) This is not to say that courts insisted that agencies must respond to each and every comment they receive. (That's a good thing, since today agencies often receive thousands of comments on important proposed rules.) But courts have insisted that especially salient or important comments receive a written response from the agency, again, in order to confirm both that the agency was actually considering the comments it received and also to ensure that the agency's ultimate regulatory result represented a reasonable decision based on all the information available to it (including, of course, the comments it received from the public).

Finally, courts began considering the consequences of a notice-and-comment process that actually succeeds in changing the agency's mind. While it might sound ironic, a rulemaking process that changes the agency's mind might require the agency to begin a new round of rulemaking. While counterintuitive, this requirement makes sense upon closer consideration. If the comments an agency receives convince it to make substantial alterations to the proposed rule, it stands to reason that interested parties should have an opportunity to comment on that new proposed rule. Otherwise, comments that might be very relevant to that altered rule— comments that point out flaws or suggest improvements—would never be heard, since, by definition, the first iteration of that rule was sufficiently different that it would not have prompted those comments.

How different are we talking about? The general approach used in the lower courts is that, if the final rule is "the logical outgrowth" of the original rule, then changes between the original and the final rule do not require an additional round of comments. The idea behind the "logical outgrowth" standard is that, if a final rule is in fact the "logical outgrowth" of the proposed rule, then interested persons did in fact enjoy an opportunity to provide relevant comments on what became the final rule. If, however, the final rule is not a "logical outgrowth" of the proposed one, then courts will conclude that those persons never had prior notice of what the agency ultimately decided to do, and thus didn't have a real chance to comment. For example, a change in the agency's methodology for calculating the magnitude of a problem, or its overall approach to how to regulate it, would likely trigger a requirement of a new comment period. By contrast, relatively minor quantitative tinkering with the originally proposed rule probably would not. Of course, these two descriptions are highly general: determinations of whether a final rule was in fact the logical outgrowth of the original one are highly fact-dependent.

2.　**Vermont Yankee**

Note that the broad interpretations of the notice-and-comment procedures discussed in the previous subsection are just that—interpretations of the statutory text. But during the 1970s courts also went farther, imposing on agencies requirements that were not even arguably required by the APA's text (or by the particular organic statute in question). For example, courts sometimes insisted that oral hearings were necessary if the issue in question was an extremely important one, or of a character that the court believed would benefit from an oral hearing.

One of these cases was *Vermont Yankee Nuclear Power Corp. v. Natural Resources Defense Council*, 435 U.S. 519 (1978). *Vermont*

Yankee involved a rulemaking by the Nuclear Regulatory Commission (NRC) regarding the safe disposal of nuclear waste. The NRC in fact provided a more formalized procedure than was required by either the APA or the nuclear regulatory statute that gave the agency the authority to act. Nevertheless, the appellate court held that the agency had provided inadequate procedures, given the extreme importance of the question of the safe disposal of nuclear waste.

The Supreme Court unanimously reversed. Justice Rehnquist explained that the APA reflected a compromise between forces that wanted to impose even more procedural requirements on agencies and those that wanted less procedure in order to allow agencies to make full use of their expertise and to be able to act quickly and effectively. He reasoned that courts had no authority to change the terms of that legislative compromise by imposing additional procedural requirements beyond those set forth in the APA.

Justice Rehnquist also set forth important practical reasons why the lower court's action was problematic. He noted that, under the lower court's approach, agencies could never be sure if they had provided enough procedures to satisfy a reviewing court, and would thus be tempted to provide the most formalized procedures possible in order to ensure against their decisions being struck down as procedurally inadequate. He also observed that the lower court's decision deeming the agency's procedures inadequate came only after the rulemaking process, at which time the court had access to information that the agency itself did not have at the start of the process, when it was deciding what procedures to follow. He described this as "Monday morning quarterbacking" that would again tempt the agency to err on the side of caution and provide more formalized procedures. Thus, he concluded, the lower court's analysis would essentially do away with the more informal notice-and-comment procedures set forth in Section 553(c). Finally, he rejected the lower court's conclusion that fuller procedures were required in order to generate the type of record that would allow the court to pass judgment on the agency's action. He concluded that Congress's provision for notice-and-comment rulemaking reflected its considered view that judicial review would be adequate even if it was based on the less robust record such a process would generate.

Vermont Yankee is important because it makes clear that courts may not go beyond the APA (or the agency's organic statute) when evaluating whether the agency provided adequate procedures to govern a rulemaking process. Nevertheless, note that cases such as *Nova Scotia*, which purported to be interpretations of the APA, remain good law. You may wish to consider whether the kind of unpredictability Justice Rehnquist worried about in *Vermont Yankee* continues to exist, with the unpredictability now centering on how aggressively a court will read the APA's rulemaking provisions. Indeed, even after *Vermont Yankee* scholars and judges continue to argue about whether the informal notice-and-comment rulemaking process has become "ossified"—that is, excessively slowed and weighted down by procedural requirements.

3. E-Rulemaking

The APA's rulemaking provisions were drafted in the 1940s, decades before the Internet. At that time, participation in a notice-and-comment rulemaking meant submitting comments by mail or personal courier, later supplemented by fax submissions. Today, it is easier than ever to participate online in most rulemakings. A website called *regulations.gov* allows anyone to search for any pending rulemaking and makes it easy to participate in that rulemaking through a few mouse clicks. You should look at *regulations.gov/* to get a sense of how easy it is.

Of course, with ease of participation come new problems unanticipated by the drafters of the APA in 1946. How much weight should a quick "I'm a citizen and I think you [the agency] should abandon/adopt this proposed rule" message carry with an agency? If the comment has no supporting information or argumentation, then one might think it should not carry a lot of weight. But what if millions of Americans send that message? Should agencies be swayed by the fact that a large number—perhaps a *very* large number—of Americans favor or oppose a regulation? Or would that be inconsistent with the agency's claim that it is the expert, and that it values only comments that help it improve on that expertise?

Other problems have also arisen with so-called "electronic rulemaking" or "e-rulemaking." For example, it's been suggested that many such "average citizen" comments are often generated by computer programs called "bots" that take over individual computers and individual computer accounts (and thus identities) and send (many) "fake" comments to agencies. But leave aside these and other similarly exotic problems. Focus instead on the fundamentals. Does electronic rulemaking change the fundamental nature of the administrative process, by providing essentially no-cost access to that process? Perhaps in an earlier era an agency could reason that anyone who was willing to go through the trouble of locating a proposed rule and submitting a comment was serious enough, committed enough, and knowledgeable enough to provide useful information. Perhaps that assumption no longer holds. Should that change how the agency approaches comments? As of today, there is no clear answer to this interesting, difficult, and important question.

D. The Choice Between Formal and Informal Rulemaking

As a general matter, courts are very hesitant to require an agency to perform formal rulemaking. Section 553(c) states that "When rules are required by statute to be made on the record after opportunity for an agency hearing, sections 556 and 557 of this title [*i.e.*, the formal rulemaking requirements set forth earlier in this chapter] apply instead of this subsection." In *United States v. Florida East Coast Railway*, 410 U.S. 224 (1973), the Supreme Court gave a very narrow reading to that provision. While the Court denied holding that formal procedures would be required only when the agency's organic statute used the precise words "on the record after opportunity for an agency hearing," it's been generally understood that, in fact, lesser language will not trigger those formal rulemaking requirements. Thus, the vast majority of rulemakings governed by the APA are informal, notice-and-comment, proceedings.

Why this reluctance to insist on formality? Part of the reason may stem from an unlikely source: peanut butter. A few years before *Florida East Coast*, the Food and Drug Administration (FDA) conducted a formal rulemaking on what seemed to be a very minor issue: whether products labelled "peanut butter" had to contain 90% peanut butter or "only" 87.5%. Those hearings turned out to be immensely long, and generated a transcript of over 7,000 pages. The experience of the peanut butter hearings was apparently well-known to judges and lawyers in Washington, and thus, of course to the Supreme Court. The obvious waste of time and resources devoted to developing information on this relatively small issue provided an obvious reason for the Court in *Florida East Coast* to not require such procedures except when Congress explicitly insisted on them. To repeat, the Court essentially held that it would only find such insistence when Congress used the precise words Section 553(c) employs as a trigger for those requirements.

The peanut butter hearings reflect a larger truth about rulemaking. Unlike adjudication, which often focuses on individualized facts, rulemaking often focuses on so-called "legislative" or "policy" facts—such as how pure peanut butter should be before, from a health and consumer protection perspective, it could be labelled "peanut butter." Such considerations require collaboration, scientific and social science fact-gathering, and policy judgment. The theory is that such functions are far better performed in an informal, collaborative internal process, supplemented by written comments (such as reports and scientific studies), rather than the highly formalized process, relying heavily on oral testimony, that characterizes formal rulemaking.

Relatedly, the reality that topics ripe for rulemaking usually implicate very large numbers of persons makes trial-type participation rights highly inefficient. Consider again the peanut butter question. A moment's reflection leads one to realize that many—indeed, millions—of American people and institutions would be interested in the question how much peanut butter has to go into a product before it can be labelled "peanut butter." Peanut farmers and wholesalers, the food companies themselves, makers of competing foods (who, for example, might want to insist on higher amounts of peanut butter in order to drive the price of that product up), and, of course, consumers would all be interested. Since formal rulemaking procedures would allow each and every person to put on witnesses, cross-examine other witnesses, take depositions, etc., one can easily imagine why such proceedings would take so long if they were conducted through formal rulemaking processes.

On this point, recall the 1915 *Bi-Metallic* case discussed in Chapter 5, which held that due process did not require a hearing when an agency altered the valuation, for property tax purposes, of all the parcels of land in a city. According to Justice Holmes, one of the reasons the Constitution did not require a hearing before that decision was that such a requirement would make it very hard for government to operate, given the large number of people who might thereby request a hearing. While *Bi-Metallic* concerned the Due

Process Clause, in contrast to *Florida East Coast*'s focus on the APA, one can hear the echoes of *Bi-Metallic* in the Court's refusal to read the APA as favoring a requirement of trial-type hearings in rulemakings.

Again, the APA allows agencies to dispense with the most extreme and futile over-proceduralization of a formal rulemaking. But the very nature of the formal rulemaking's default *in favor* of formality necessarily means that such procedures will likely be long and arduous. That fact, when combined with the fact that most of the relevant information useful to a policy determination—*e.g.*, how much of a given pollutant is safe for drinking water, or how much peanut butter should be required to go into something labelled "peanut butter"—can be obtained through written sources, has led courts largely to shy away from imposing formal rulemaking requirements upon agencies.

E. Hybrid Rulemaking

The previous discussion of the agency's discretion to choose between formal and informal rulemaking should not lead you to think that the only possible sets of procedures for rulemaking are the "formal" and "informal" rulemaking procedures the APA sets out. As we've noted several times, the APA provides only the default rules that apply if Congress has not provided more specific procedures for an agency's administration of a particular statute. Sometimes Congress does indeed provide a specific set of procedures for a given agency to follow when administering a particular program. Often, those procedures take the form of a combination of the APA's formal and informal procedures. Such procedures are called "hybrid" procedures. This short guide focusing on general principles of federal administrative law cannot provide an exhaustive discussion of every substantive statute that provides for such hybrid procedures. For our purposes, the most important thing to take away is that, when determining what procedures an agency must follow, it is crucial to examine the agency's organic statute, to make sure Congress did not prescribe a set of procedures that were intended to supplant the APA's default procedures.

F. Negotiated Rulemaking

In the Negotiated Rulemaking Act, Congress gave agencies some limited authority to convene a committee of interested private parties to help it negotiate a proposed rule. The proposed rule is then subjected to the standard notice-and-comment process. The hope of negotiated rulemaking is that all major sides of an issue would have reached a negotiated consensus on what a rule should be, which, it is hoped, would make the notice-and-comment process quicker and less contentious. It is also hoped that such a process would forestall legal challenges to the final rule.

As you might imagine, such negotiated processes might be more successful in some contexts than in others. For example, it might be harder for interested parties to reach a negotiated consensus when they have hard-and-fast and diametrically opposed positions, or where negotiating power is lopsided, such that the weaker party feels it is not getting a fair deal, or when one side or the other feels like the law is clearly on their side such that the chances for victory in litigation are high.

The short version: Formal rulemaking involves oral presentation and trial-type procedures, while informal rulemaking contemplates simply a process in which interested persons submit written comments on the proposed rule. Due to the collegial, policy-based nature of rulemaking, courts will require formal rulemaking only when the organic statute uses the exact or something very close to the exact words the APA uses to trigger a requirement of formality. Despite its seeming informality, courts have interpreted the APA's informal rulemaking requirements as imposing significant procedural hurdles on agencies. The Supreme Court has ruled that courts have no authority to impose additional procedural requirements beyond those in the APA or the agency's organic statute.

CHAPTER 7

Exceptions to the Rulemaking Process

Not all rulemakings governed by the APA have to follow the APA's rulemaking procedures. Section 553 of the APA sets forth an intricate structure of exceptions to the rulemaking processes laid out in Chapter 6. Subsection (a) exempts from all of Section 553's requirements rules relating to "military or foreign affairs" functions, and those "relating to agency management or personnel or to public property, loans, grants, benefits, or contracts." Section 553 also exempts other types of rules from some, but not all, of its requirements.

- "Interpretive rules" and "statements of policy" are exempt from both the notice requirement of subsection (b) and the pre-effective date publication requirement of subsection (d). Note that being exempt from the notice requirement of subsection (b) effectively means that such rules are also exempt from the participation rights provided in subsection (c). In other words, if the action in question is

exempt from the "notice" requirement it is also
exempt from the "comment" requirement.

- In addition, if the "agency for good cause finds that
notice and public procedure thereon are
impracticable, unnecessary, or contrary to the
public interest," then the rule is again exempt from
subsection (b)'s notice (and thus subsection (c)'s
comment) requirements. In addition, this "good
cause" provision exempts a rule from subsection
(d)'s pre-effective date publication requirement.

- Finally, "rules of agency organization, procedure, or
practice" are exempt from subsection (b)'s notice
(and thus subsection (c)'s comment) requirements.
However, such "procedural rules" are *not* exempt
from (that is, they *must comply with*) subsection
(d)'s pre-effective date publication requirement.

The rest of this chapter fleshes out the definitions of each of these
types of rules.

A. Foreign Affairs and Military Functions

Section 553(a) completely exempts rules pertaining to foreign
affairs and military functions from the requirements of the rest of
that section. The logic is straightforward: such rules may involve
sensitive national security concerns, which militate against
requiring the agency to go through a notice-and-comment process,
provide advance notice of such rules, and allow persons to request
the agency to amend or repeal such rules.

B. Rules "Relating to Agency Management or Personnel or to Public Property, Loans, Grants, Benefits, or Contracts"

At first glance one might think that this exception makes good, straightforward sense, since it seems to deal with internal agency housekeeping issues. But note that in the modern world "loans," "grants," "benefits," and "contracts" involving the government are immensely important to millions of people. Indeed, rules about something as important as Social Security would seem to come within this exception. It's been suggested that Congress's decision to exempt such rules from notice and comment reflected the idea, prevalent in 1946 when the APA was enacted, that such items were mere governmental "gratuities" and thus did not require a great deal of process. As you'll see when you learn about due process in Chapter 13, this idea has now been rejected; today, benefits such as Social Security and veterans' benefits are thought to be every bit as important as interests more strongly protected under traditional due process jurisprudence. Indeed, the Social Security statute explicitly subjects rules implementing that program to notice-and-comment rulemaking, as do many other statutes involving programs that would otherwise come within this exception.

C. The "Good Cause" Exception

The APA allows agencies to avoid Section 553's notice and comment requirement, and the requirement that rules be published in the *Federal Register* 30 days before their effective date, when the agency finds "good cause" for avoiding those requirements. The particular exemption from the notice and comment requirement is phrased more specifically, to apply when notice and comment is "impracticable, unnecessary, or contrary to the public interest."

This exemption is a straightforward allowance to the agency to not comply with the relevant parts of Section 553 when the agency believes there is good reason not to comply with those requirements. Courts have concluded that such compliance is "impracticable" when, for example, there is a strong need for the agency to act quickly to avoid a public health or safety problem. They have found compliance "unnecessary" when the rule in question is insignificant. Finally, they have found compliance "contrary to the public interest" when, for example, compliance would incentivize regulated parties to rush to engage in soon-to-be prohibited conduct, thus exacerbating the situation the agency sought to remedy.

Nevertheless, agencies do not get a free pass when they cite the good cause exemption. An agency must demonstrate why this exemption applies.

D. "Procedural Rules"

At one level, a procedural rule is easy to define by contrasting it to a "substantive" rule. Intuitively, you might have a sense of the difference between substance and process. But you probably also know from Civil Procedure that it's very difficult to draw a clear line between substance and procedure, given how the most procedural-sounding provision (*e.g.*, a pleading rule) can have a significant effect on the substantive outcome of a case.

The same difficulty complicates attempts to define a "rule of agency organization, procedure, or practice" (which we can shorthand as a "procedural rule"). As noted in the prior paragraph, it is insufficient to say that a procedural rule is a rule that doesn't impact (or directly impact) substance.

Probably the best attempt courts have made to define "procedural rules" for purposes of Section 553's exceptions teaches that a procedural rule is a rule that does not encode a substantive value judgment. In other words, a procedural rule is one that does not reflect an agency's particular substantive policy preference. This definition was announced in a case called *Public Citizen v. Department of State*, 276 F.3d 634 (D.C. Cir. 2002). That case dealt with the Freedom of Information Act (FOIA), which requires agencies to disclose information it possesses in response to private requests. (FOIA is discussed in Chapter 25.) The State Department promulgated a rule that said, basically, that a FOIA request received on a given date would trigger an agency duty to search for responsive documents *that were created on or before that date*. For example, a FOIA request received on June 30, 2021, would require the agency to search for responsive documents created on June 30, 2021 or before—it would not require the agency to search for documents created on July 1 or later, even though the agency's search for responsive documents would extend well past July 1.

Clearly, this rule had a substantive impact on FOIA requesters—that is, it imposed more burdens on them, by requiring them to submit additional FOIA requests if they wanted more recent documents. But the court concluded that because there was no substantive value judgment reflected in the rule it was procedural for purposes of Section 553's exceptions structure. In other words, the challenged rule did not, for example, reflect a substantive preference for some FOIA requests over others, but was simply a neutral way for the agency to decide how to manage all the FOIA requests it received.

To be sure, the "encoding a substantive value judgment" principle isn't perfect. After all, in *Public Citizen* the agency's rule *did* reflect a judgment to make life harder for FOIA requesters. Nevertheless, the test has become an influential one.

E. "Interpretive Rules" and "Policy Statements"

Now that we have dealt with the exceptions in subsection (a), the "good cause" exception, and the exemption for "procedural rules," we will now consider Section 553's exceptions for "interpretive rules" and "policy statements." Begin with what these types of rules are *not*: they are not "legislative rules." What's a legislative rule? Simply put, a legislative rule is a rule that makes law, and is thus legally binding. In other words, a legislative rule is a rule that changes the law in some way, and thus is not, for example, a rule that merely interprets a pre-existing rule. Second, a legislative rule is legally binding, rather than being, say, a rule that merely states the agency's general view about how it will approach its regulatory task (which, as we'll see, is called a "policy statement").

Such non-legislative rules (interpretive rules and policy statements) are very useful for persons subject to an agency's regulation (for example, stockbrokers subject to SEC regulations). Interpretive rules give such persons guidance about how an agency understands a particular statute or legislative rule. As such, they can help such persons steer clear of actions the agency might consider illegal. Similarly, policy statements can give such persons a sense of what types of legal violations the agency considers to be most serious, so they can make sure to conform their conduct accordingly. It can be very helpful for an agency to provide this guidance quickly and informally, without having to go through the formalities of notice-and-comment rulemaking or having to provide 30 days' notice before its effective date. (Indeed, it might even be thought incoherent to require such notice, since what we're talking about is, for example, the agency's already-existing understanding of what a rule means or how it will likely approach its enforcement duties.)

At the same time, an agency's ability to avoid notice-and-comment procedures might tempt it to describe a legislative rule as, instead, an interpretive rule or a policy statement. As we will see, there are no clear lines between legislative rules on the one hand, and interpretive rules or policy statements on the other. This will often give agencies an incentive to avoid notice and comment rulemaking. This possibility is discussed in subsection (3), below.

1. *Interpretive Rules*

At one level, it should be clear what an "interpretive" rule is— it's a rule that, literally, interprets another rule (or a statutory provision), rather than a legislative rule. But that seeming clarity evaporates when one realizes that an interpretation (say, of a legislative rule) can easily be understood as imposing new legal requirements—that is, as a legislative rule in its own right. Consider one example. A federal mine safety regulation requires mine owners to forward to the agency any "diagnoses" of mining-related illnesses that it becomes aware of in one of its workers. Then, the agency states that mine owners must turn over x-rays of miners when those x-rays reveal a certain medical condition common to miners. Is that latter requirement merely an interpretation of the "diagnosis" rule, or a new legislative rule? *See American Mining Congress v. Mine Safety & Health Administration*, 995 F.2d 1106 (D.C. Cir. 1993) (confronting this fact pattern).

Given this ambiguity, it should not be surprising that there is no clear way to distinguish between interpretive rules and legislative rules. But one can still discern some basic principles. First, if an agency explicitly invokes its legislative rule-making power, then the result should be considered a legislative rule. Second, if, in the absence of the claimed interpretive rule there would be no rule of conduct for regulated parties to follow, then again, the rule would be legislative. This latter situation would occur if, for example, the agency's organic statute simply authorized the agency to promulgate regulations rather than itself prohibiting or regulating particular conduct. In such a case there would be, literally, nothing for the alleged interpretive rule to interpret, at least until the agency promulgated a legislative rule, which then in turn could be the subject of an interpretive rule. Third, if the rule amends or repeals a legislative rule, it itself should be considered a legislative rule.

If a regulation cannot be characterized in any of these ways, and if the regulation is at least arguably an interpretation of some other rule of conduct (either a regulation or the organic statute itself) then it's likely that the regulation will be deemed interpretive. Indeed, in *American Mining Congress*, the case cited earlier in this discussion, the court applied these principles. It observed that the agency had not invoked its rulemaking authority, and noted that the underlying "diagnosis" rule presented a possible subject of an interpretive rule. Finally, it concluded that the x-ray rule could be understood as consistent with the underlying "diagnosis" rule, and thus did not have to be understood as amending (let alone repealing) that rule. Thus, the court concluded that the x-ray rule was in fact an interpretive rule.

2. *Policy Statements*

Finally, "general statements of policy" are exempt from Section 553's notice-and-comment and pre-effective date publication requirements. The *Attorney General's Manual on the APA*, a document drafted by the Attorney General very shortly after the APA was enacted and an influential source of the APA's meaning, defines such statements as those "issued by an agency to advise the public prospectively of the manner in which the agency proposes to exercise a discretionary power."

A key feature of policy statements is that they are non-binding: that is, they simply reflect the agency's general understanding of how it will use the powers its organic statute grants it. Thus, for example, if an agency strictly follows a position it has taken in an alleged policy statement, a court may determine that the so-called policy statement is actually a legislative rule. Consider, for example, *United States Telephone Association v. FCC*, 28 F.3d 1232 (D.C. Cir. 1994). In *United States Telephone*, the agency announced the base penalty levels it would assess when finding particular types of regulatory violations, and the factors that it would consider in deciding whether to deviate from those levels. The agency argued that that statement was simply a statement of the agency's general enforcement policy, insisting in the statement that it retained discretion to deviate from that policy. The court disagreed, and found that the statement was in fact a legislative rule (which thus should have gone through notice-and-comment) in part because it appeared that, in fact, the agency almost never deviated from those base levels. The court also noted that the so-called policy was too detailed and specific to be considered simply a general statement of the agency's enforcement approach.

As you can imagine, the line between a genuine policy statement that an agency just happens to follow a lot and a legislative rule is quite blurry. After all, a policy statement is *designed* to reflect the agency's views on a particular issue; thus, it's not surprising (or problematic) when the agency ends up following those views on a regular basis. As with interpretive rules, this ambiguity often means that agencies will be able to avoid the notice-and-comment requirements if it wishes to do so.

3. *Agency Incentives*

Given the murkiness of the distinctions between legislative rules on the one hand and, on the other, interpretive rules and policy statements, and given also the leeway agencies might seem to enjoy to avoid having to call something a legislative rule (and thus have to go through notice-and-comment rulemaking), you might ask why agencies don't use these exceptions even more. To be sure, they do use these exceptions—a lot. But courts have suggested that there may be incentives for agencies not to abuse this leeway. Most importantly, when an interpretive rule or policy statement is challenged in court, an agency may have a harder time convincing the court that the rule is reasonable if it can't show that it solicited input from regulated parties. Such a failure might convince a court that the agency lacked all the relevant information that was available, and thus reached a sub-standard conclusion. By contrast, an agency might have an easier time defending the reasonableness of a *legislative* rule—i.e., one that went through notice-and-comment—exactly because the notice-and-comment process revealed to the agency all of the relevant information.

Second, a legislative rule—exactly because it is "legislative" (in the sense that it explicitly makes law)—is binding on all persons. This fact may mean that a legislative rule will win broader compliance with less agency effort. The theory here is that regulated parties will be less tempted to take their chances on the agency filing an enforcement action against them, since the (legislative) regulation is already binding on them, in contrast to a mere interpretive rule, which, since it's not legally binding on its own force, does not formally apply to any party until an enforcement action is brought.

To be sure, both of these benefits—the relatively greater likelihood that a court will uphold a legislative rule and the increased chance of gaining broad industry compliance from promulgating such a rule—come at the cost of having to go through the notice-and-comment process. As we saw in Chapter 6, that process can be onerous, even when it's of the informal, notice-and-comment, variety. But courts have speculated that on some occasions these benefits may make it worthwhile for the agency to embark on the notice-and-comment path, and to avoid taking advantage of either of these exceptions.

The short version: There are a number of types of rules that are exempt from some or all of the APA's rulemaking requirements. The most important of these types of rules are "procedural" rules, "interpretive" rules, "general statements of [agency] policy," and rules for which there is "good cause" to avoid a rulemaking process. Each of these types of exempted rules can be identified via tests particular to that type of rule.

CHAPTER 8

Ex Parte Contacts and Bias in Rulemaking

A basic requirement of a fair process—of any sort—is that there be no back channel, or *"ex parte"* communications: that is, everything is done on a public record. Another basic requirement is that the decision-maker be unbiased. However, some government activities, including rulemaking, are of the sort that these requirements are difficult to honor entirely.

A. *Ex Parte* Communications

The APA does not have any provisions prohibiting *ex parte* communications in informal, notice-and-comment rulemaking. (As discussed later in this section, it does prohibit some *ex parte* communications when the agency is engaging in *formal* rulemaking.) Nevertheless, in the 1970s some courts suggested that *ex parte* communications should be prohibited, given the fundamental unfairness of a process that features such communications, and given also that such communications render the eventual rule substantively problematic, since commenters excluded from such communications lacked a chance to engage the arguments made during those private communications.

One notable case of this sort is *Home Box Office v. Federal Communications Commission*, 567 F.2d 9 (D.C. Cir. 1977). *Home Box Office* dealt with a rulemaking in which the agency engaged in significant *ex parte* discussions with members of a particular interest group. The court, expressing the concerns identified in the prior paragraph, struck the rulemaking down. In addition to noting the problems identified above, it also expressed concern that, when the rule was challenged in court as substantively arbitrary, the court would not be able to perform its judicial review role because it wouldn't know what really motivated the agency to act as it did, given the existence of *ex parte* communications disclosed neither to the general public nor to the court.

Such attempts to impose restrictions on *ex parte* communications in informal rulemaking were dealt a blow when the Supreme Court decided, in *Vermont Yankee Nuclear Power Corp. v. Natural Resources Defense Council*, 435 U.S. 519 (1978), that courts lacked the power to impose procedural requirements on agencies that were not found either in the APA or the agency's organic statute. (*Vermont Yankee* is discussed in more detail in Chapter 6.) To be sure, courts have continued to observe that, if a rulemaking appears quasi-adjudicatory in nature, due process might require restrictions on *ex parte* contacts, even if the APA does not. (A rulemaking might be adjudicatory in nature if, to use some courts' terminology, it involves "competing private claims to a valuable privilege"—for example, if the agency, by regulation, decides which entity or type of entity will be allowed to access a particular benefit that cannot be easily shared.) But, in other situations, *ex parte* communications will not be prohibited when an agency engages in informal rulemaking.

Formal rulemaking is another matter. In 1976, Congress amended the APA. One of the changes was to impose limits on agencies' *ex parte* communications *with persons outside the agency* when the agency engages in either formal rulemaking or formal adjudication. Codified mainly at Section 557(d), these provisions prohibit both agencies and such external persons from having *ex parte* contacts with each other, and require that, if such contacts are made, their substance be placed on the formal rulemaking record. Importantly, Section 557(d) raises the specter that a party knowingly violating these prohibitions could find its "claim or interest in the proceeding . . . dismissed, denied, disregarded, or otherwise adversely affected on account of such violation." (Section 556(d) also includes a provision raising this same threat.)

Note that these prohibitions pertain only to *external ex parte* contacts: even in formal rulemaking, agency personnel can continue to speak among themselves *ex parte*. This latitude is often explained as reflecting the reality of the rulemaking process, which is understood as a process in which different agency personnel (*e.g.*, lawyers, policy experts, and technical experts) must be able to talk and share information informally in order to develop the best rule.

Finally, note that while Section 557(d) applies to both formal rulemaking and formal adjudication, additional restrictions on *ex parte* contacts—restrictions on the decision-maker's communications with personnel *inside* the agency—apply to formal adjudications (but not to rulemaking, either informal or formal). These restrictions on *internal ex parte* contacts (which again, apply only to formal adjudications) are discussed in Chapter 14, which considers integrity issues in adjudications.

B. Bias and Prejudgment

The same character of the rulemaking process identified above—that is, its character as a collegial process in which different agency personnel need to speak informally about the relevant issues—has also been cited as a reason to not impose a sharp requirement that an agency not be biased about, or not have prejudged, a particular regulatory issue. The standard rule regarding such bias or prejudgment is that the agency not have "an unalterably closed mind" or "an irrevocably closed mind" about the question. This is a difficult standard for plaintiffs to meet. The reason for that is that one would *expect* the agency to have pre-existing views about a particular regulatory issue before it sets about promulgating a rule on that issue. Indeed, it would be odd— even problematic—for the agency to commence a rulemaking without having any pre-judged idea at all about whether the particular subject required regulation or whether the proposed regulation in question was a good idea. At the same time, there needs to be some guarantee that the agency has not so irrevocably prejudged the issue that the public rulemaking process is a mere formality, which is guaranteed not to change the agency's mind. This balance is reflected in the requirement that the agency not have an "unalterably" or "irrevocably" "closed mind."

One example of this situation arose in *Association of National Advertisers v. Federal Trade Commission*, 627 F.2d 1151 (D.C. Cir. 1979). In *National Advertisers*, a coalition of marketers and advertising agencies sued the agency when it proposed a rule limiting advertising aimed at children. The plaintiffs argued that the agency head was illegally biased in favor of the content of the proposed rule, given public statements he had made about the general problem of such advertising and its potential to mislead. The court concluded that such a challenge could succeed only if the plaintiffs had proven by "clear and convincing evidence" that the agency head had "an unalterably closed mind." In adopting such a high standard for the plaintiffs to meet, the court explained that the very nature of the rulemaking process was such that agency personnel had to be expected to have discussed the policy issues relevant to a rulemaking before proposing a rule. That discussion in turn would likely have given those personnel some opinions about the wisdom of the rule. The "unalterably closed mind" test respects that reality, while at the same time ensuring that the ensuing rulemaking process is meaningful by ensuring that agency personnel remain open to having their opinions changed by the information commenters present.

The short version: Informal rulemaking is not subject to any APA-based limits on *ex parte* communications. By contrast, the APA does limit an agency's *ex parte* contacts in formal rulemaking, but only *ex parte* contacts with persons *outside* the agency. The nature of rulemaking is such that both informal and formal rulemaking is subject to only very limited restrictions on an agency decision-maker's prejudgment of the policy or social facts that are usually at issue in rulemakings: as long as the agency does not have an "unalterably" or "irrevocably" closed mind, such prejudgment claims will fail.

CHAPTER 9

White House Review of Rulemaking

In addition to the rulemaking requirements imposed by statutes (the APA and agencies' organic statutes) and the remaining congressional oversight tools discussed in Chapter 4, agencies are also subject to White House review of their proposed rules. Starting with President Reagan in 1981 and continuing to the present day, presidents have promulgated executive orders requiring agencies to submit proposed regulations to a White House office—the Office of Management and Budget (OMB)—for review.

The details of these orders have often changed with changes in presidential administrations, but the basics have remained consistent. Under these executive orders, agencies must submit proposed and final regulations to OMB, and explain how those regulations balance regulatory costs and benefits. More recent versions of these orders have made clear that OMB does not have the authority to order the agency to do anything in response to OMB's review. In particular, they make clear that such proposed regulations must remain consistent with the directives the agency received in the organic statute that gave the agency the authority to promulgate those regulations in the first place. Thus, for example, if an organic statute directed the agency to promulgate regulations to take care of a particular problem regardless of the cost, an agency cannot be required by OMB to change its regulation to reflect a cost-benefit analysis. The point of this regulatory review is to ensure that the White House is able to influence (even if it's not able to dictate) the regulatory output of that administration and to ensure to the extent possible that that output is consistent with the President's overall priorities and implemented as cost effectively as possible.

The regulatory review noted above has often been limited to executive agencies, rather than extending to so-called "independent agencies" (which are discussed in Chapter 3). Another feature of these executive orders is the requirement that agencies submit to the White House an annual regulatory agenda—that is, a statement of the agency's plan for what regulations it is planning on promulgating that year. Similar to OMB review of individual proposed regulations, this requirement is designed to ensure that the agency's overall regulatory agenda for the coming year is consistent with the President's priorities. Some presidents have sought to impose the regulatory agenda requirement on both executive branch and independent agencies.

The short version: Since the 1980s, presidents have issued executive orders requiring agencies to consult with a White House office, the Office of Management and Budget (OMB), when issuing proposed or final regulations. The main goal of this consultation requirement is to ensure that agencies are acting consistently with the President's priorities when they implement the statutes for which they have responsibility.

* * * * *

THE TAKEAWAY

What are the main issues this Part addresses?

- **The distinction between rulemaking and adjudication.**

  As a very general matter, one can analogize rulemaking to legislation and adjudication to court action. Only adjudications are subject to the protections of the Due Process Clause.

- **The agency's discretion to choose between employing rulemaking and adjudication.**

  The agency has broad discretion to choose, subject to very limited conditions.

- **The procedures required for formal and informal rulemaking.**

  Formal rulemaking requires something akin to trial-type procedures, including a decision based on the formal record and, in most cases, an opportunity for oral presentation. Informal rulemaking entails a process in which interested parties are allowed to submit written comments on a proposed agency regulation.

- **The circumstances under which an agency must engage in formal rulemaking.**

  Agencies must engage in formal rulemaking only under very limited circumstances; essentially, when the organic statute uses the precise words specified in the APA for such formality: "on the record after opportunity for an agency hearing."

- **The types of rules that are exempt from the rulemaking process.**

  Procedural rules, interpretive rules, policy statements, and rules for which there is good cause to avoid such procedures are the main categories of rules exempt from some or all of the APA's rulemaking procedures.

- **The integrity rules that apply to rulemaking.**

  Due to the nature of the rulemaking function, informal rulemaking is subject to no rules restricting *ex parte* contacts, and few restrictions on agency prejudgment. Formal rulemaking is subject to APA-based rules restricting *ex parte* contacts with personnel *outside* the agency.

- **White House review of rulemaking.**

  Since the 1980s, presidents have issued executive orders mandating White House review of proposed and final agency regulations. These orders acknowledge the agency's ultimate legal authority to act, based on the agency's organic statute.

Agency Adjudication

This part of the *Guide* covers agency adjudicative procedures. Recall that Chapter 2 set forth the rules governing the constitutionality of statutory schemes that authorized agencies to adjudicate. Part Three focuses on the procedures that an agency must follow when performing such adjudications. Chapter 10 provides an overview of adjudicative processes. Chapter 11 considers the agency's discretion to choose between formal and informal adjudicative processes. Chapter 12 considers those formal processes, while Chapter 13 considers the Due Process Clause, which provides most (though not all) of the procedural requirements for informal adjudication. Chapter 14 concludes this Part by examining integrity issues in adjudication.

CHAPTER 10

An Overview of Adjudication Procedures

The APA prescribes procedures for formal adjudication and, to a much lesser degree, informal adjudication. That gap—that is, the APA's failure to provide significant procedural guideposts for informal adjudication—is filled in by the Due Process Clause of the Fifth Amendment.

The APA's procedures for formal adjudication are provided in Sections 554, 556, and 557. (Recall from Chapter 6 that Sections 556 and 557 also apply to formal rulemaking; however, Section 554 applies only to formal adjudication.) Sections 556 and 557 lay out a series of requirements and procedures that reflect the trial-type nature of formal adjudications (and formal rulemakings). Among other things, Section 556 provides for recusals of decision-makers (subsection (b)), sets forth the powers of the presiding officer, which include a variety of tasks that reflect that trial-type nature (including administering oaths, issuing subpoenas, regulating depositions, and ruling on settlement offers) (subsection (c)), and provides for oral testimony and cross-examination and requires that all decisions be based on the record (respectively, subsections (d) and (e)). For its part, Section 557 provides that the decision of an ALJ constitutes the decision of the agency unless the agency head hears an appeal (subsection (b)), gives parties the chance to submit proposed findings and conclusions and to submit objections to any tentative agency findings or conclusions (subsection (c)), and restricts *ex parte* contacts between the agency decision-maker and persons outside the agency (subsection (d)). Chapter 6 provides additional detail about Sections 556 and 557. You should review that material now.

The procedures above apply to both formal rulemaking and formal adjudication. Section 554, which applies only to formal adjudication, provides, among other things, the procedural rules that are uniquely relevant to agency adjudication (subsection (b)), and, in subsection (d), the rules regulating the independence of agency adjudicators from agency prosecutors and investigators as well as the rules regulating the adjudicator's ability to communicate *ex parte* with other persons inside the agency.

By contrast to this panoply of rules and procedures governing formal adjudication, the APA says very little about the procedures for *informal* adjudications. In *Pension Benefit Guarantee Corp. v. LTV Corp.*, 496 U.S. 633 (1990), the Court concluded that Section 706 of the APA, which authorizes courts to strike down agency action that is "arbitrary and capricious," imposes a minimal procedural requirement that agencies offer explanations for their decisions sufficient to provide a foundation for "arbitrary and capricious" review. (The "arbitrary and capricious" standard, and the other standards courts employ to review agency action, are discussed later, in Part Five.) The Court also noted that Section 555 also provides a set of minimal procedural requirements applicable to informal adjudications. Probably the most important of these latter requirements is Section 555(e)'s provision that the agency's notice of a denial of a person's petition, application, or other request be accompanied by "a brief statement of the grounds for denial."

Given the relative paucity of procedural requirements for informal adjudication, the Due Process Clause of the Fifth Amendment plays an important role in setting forth the procedures required when an agency performs such adjudication. By contrast, the robustness of the procedures required by formal adjudication means that, as a practical matter, the Due Process Clause will not play an important independent role when the agency engages in formal adjudication. The Due Process Clause is discussed in Chapter 13.

Before we continue our discussion of adjudication, let's pause and take stock. The following chart sets forth the sources of law governing the procedural requirements agencies must follow when they engage in rulemaking and adjudication.

Table 1:   Procedural Requirements for
Rulemaking and Adjudication

	Rulemaking	Adjudication
Formal	APA Sections 553 (subsections (b), (d), and (e)), and Sections 556 & 557	APA Sections 554, 556, and 557
Informal	APA Section 553	APA Sections 555 and 706; Due Process Clause

Note one caveat to this chart. The Due Process Clause applies to formal adjudication (the upper right box) as well as informal adjudication (the lower right box). But the upper right box doesn't include the Due Process Clause because, as noted earlier, the procedural requirements of APA Sections 554, 556, and 557 likely satisfy any requirement that due process would impose. The same is true of APA Sections 555 and 706: again, technically, those sections apply to formal adjudication as well as to informal adjudication, but their requirements would almost necessarily be satisfied by the formal adjudication procedures set forth in Sections 554, 556, and 557.

The short version: The APA provides relatively minimal requirements for informal adjudication, in Sections 555 and 706, with the main procedural requirements for such adjudication flowing from the Due Process Clause. By contrast, Sections 554, 556, and 557 provide a detailed set of trial-type procedures when an agency acts via formal adjudication.

CHAPTER 11

The Choice Between Formal and Informal Adjudication

As with rulemaking, an agency may sometimes be forced to comply with the requirements of the APA's formal adjudication provisions, while in other cases the agency may be free to act informally, subject only to the minimal requirements set forth in the APA plus whatever may be required by the Due Process Clause. The language triggering the requirements of formal adjudication is the same as the language triggering the requirements of formal rulemaking. In both cases, formality is required if the agency's organic statute requires the agency to act "on the record after opportunity for an agency hearing." You'll recall from Chapter 6 that, in the rulemaking context, this language appears in Section 553(c). For adjudications, you can find that language in Section 554(a).

Interestingly, however, courts have read that language differently in the two contexts. As noted in Chapter 6, the Supreme Court has all-but required that, in order for formal rulemaking to be required, Congress must use the exact words from the APA—*i.e.*,

Congress must require that the agency promulgate regulations "on the record after opportunity for an agency hearing." By contrast, courts have not uniformly adopted this strict requirement in the context of adjudication. (In the adjudication context, the law has been made by the federal appellate courts, as the Supreme Court has never conclusively weighed in on the question.) Some appellate courts have adopted the Supreme Court's analogous approach to rulemaking, holding that agencies are presumed to be allowed to use informal adjudicative methods unless Congress uses the exact words from the APA. But other appellate courts have adopted the exact opposite presumption, holding that agencies are presumed to be required to use *formal* adjudicative procedures unless Congress clearly allows a less formal process. Finally, some courts have applied the Supreme Court's general rule that agencies merit deference when they provide a reasonable interpretation of a vague provision in their organic statute. (In this context, the provision would be the one governing the formality of the adjudication procedures they must follow.) Note, though, that this latter approach essentially gives the agency the discretion to choose informality, since it requires courts to defer to an agency's decision to use informal procedures whenever the statute is unclear on the question. (Technically, that deference would also extend to an agency's decision that its organic statute requires *formal* procedures, but it would be a rare—maybe an impossible—case in which an agency chooses formal procedures but is challenged by a party who insists that the statute requires *informality*.) This latter approach is based on the so-called "*Chevron* doctrine," which is discussed in Chapter 22.

Why this diversity of viewpoints regarding adjudication procedures, in the face of the Supreme Court's aversion to formality in rulemaking? It may be because courts (including the Supreme Court) likely believe that informality is inherently appropriate for rulemaking, because rulemaking is viewed as an inherently collegial process, and one that focuses on broad policy facts rather than facts about a particular individual. (Recall the discussion of this point in Chapter 6.) By contrast, courts may instinctively prefer formality when the agency engages in adjudication, on the theory that adjudication by its very nature implicates a single party who should therefore have strong rights to participate, in a formal way, in the process by which her liability is adjudicated. This idea implicates the distinction between the *Londoner* and *Bi-Metallic* cases, discussed in Chapter 5. Regardless of the reason, the law governing the agency's discretion to choose between formal and informal adjudication is not as clear-cut as the analogous law in the rulemaking context.

The short version: Unlike rulemaking, where courts strain to read statutory language to allow the agency to use informal procedures, courts will sometimes read statutory language to require formal procedures in adjudication. The lower courts are split on this issue, and the Supreme Court has not decided this question conclusively.

CHAPTER 12

Formal Adjudication

Formal adjudication is governed by Sections 554, 556, and 557 of the APA. The latter two of these sections also apply to formal rulemaking; these sections were explained in Chapter 6, to which you should now refer. (Note that when you read that material you'll find one provision, in Section 556(d), that applies to formal rulemaking but not formal adjudication; otherwise, Sections 556 and 557 apply to both formal rulemaking and formal adjudication.)

While Sections 556 and 557 apply to both formal rulemaking and formal adjudication, Section 554 applies only to formal adjudication, and thus is discussed here. Much of Section 554 is devoted to the procedural details that attend adjudications as contrasted to rulemakings. Thus, for example, Section 554(b) states that:

"Persons entitled to notice of an agency hearing shall be timely informed of—

(1) the time, place, and nature of the hearing;

(2) the legal authority and jurisdiction under which the hearing is to be held; and

(3)   the matters of fact and law asserted."

This provision reflects the difference between adjudications—which affect particular parties—and rulemakings—which affect entire classes of persons—by making clear that notice of an adjudication shall be more particularized, to "persons entitled to notice" of that hearing.

More substantively, Section 554(c) speaks to the rights participants in a formal hearing have. It provides:

"(c) The agency shall give all interested parties opportunity for—

(1) the submission and consideration of facts, arguments, offers of settlement, or proposals of adjustment when time, the nature of the proceeding, and the public interest permit; and

(2) to the extent that the parties are unable so to determine a controversy by consent, hearing and decision on notice and in accordance with sections 556 and 557 of this title."

Subsection (c)(2) simply points toward Sections 556 and 557 as describing the type of hearing to which parties have a right when the adjudication is a formal one. Subsection (c)(1) again reflects the adjudicative nature of the proceeding, by giving parties not just the opportunity to submit "facts" and "arguments," but also "offers of settlement" and "proposals of adjustment."

Finally, subsection (d) limits the agency adjudicator's ability to engage in *ex parte* contacts with personnel inside the agency. This issue is treated in Chapter 14, which deals generally with issues of *ex parte* contacts in adjudication.

The short version: The APA's formal adjudication procedures provide a detailed set of procedural requirements. Those requirements reflect the trial-type nature of formal adjudication, and also insist that the agency's decision be based solely on the formal record created during that process.

CHAPTER 13

Due Process

As set forth in Chapter 10 (see Table 1 of that Chapter), the APA says relatively little about the procedures agencies must follow when they engage in informal adjudication. Instead, the Due Process Clauses of the Constitution provide the most important generally-applicable procedural guidelines for informal adjudication. (The caveat "generally applicable" is included because, as always, the agency's organic statute can prescribe particular procedures for adjudications performed under that particular regulatory program.) The Fifth and Fourteenth Amendments to the Constitution both contain guarantees that, respectively, neither the Federal Government nor any state shall "deprive any person of life, liberty, or property without due process of law." You probably studied the Due Process Clauses of both of these amendments in Constitutional Law. At that point, you may have studied only their substantive aspects—that is, their guarantee of particular substantive rights, such as the right to an abortion, the right to contraceptives, and the right to sexual autonomy. (From this point on, this *Guide* will refer to the Due Process Clause in the singular.)

In administrative law, the procedural aspect of the Due Process Clause asks not about whether government is *substantively* justified in depriving an individual of the right in question, but instead about whether it has followed constitutionally adequate *procedures* in doing so. This is a particularly important question in administrative law, because government acts in many ways that infringe on interests protected by the due process guarantee. (As you'll see shortly, many more interests enjoy meaningful protection under this procedural guarantee than under the substantive aspects of the Due Process Clause.) Our examination of these procedural aspects will consider three questions, each of which will provide the foundation for the next question:

1. Is the interest in question a "life, liberty, or property" interest that is protected by the Due Process Clause?

2. If it is, has government "deprived" the individual of that interest?

3. If it has, has it provided constitutionally adequate process?

A. Identifying Interests That Are Protected by the Due Process Clause

The Due Process Clause protects against deprivations of "life, liberty, and property." In some contexts these terms have clearly identifiable applications. If an immigration agency detains someone at the border, it has deprived that person of her liberty. If an agency seizes a businessperson's inventory (for example, an inventory of food items claimed to be unsafe), it has deprived that person of her property.

A quick word about "life." Generally speaking, we don't speak of agencies depriving persons of their lives, although that is theoretically possible. But the context of most situations in which governments deprive persons of life—capital punishment for a crime—comes freighted with many procedural protections provided by other provisions of the Bill of Rights. Thus, procedural objections to capital punishment (*e.g.*, the argument that the defendant was deprived of the assistance of counsel) usually rest on those more specific Bill of Rights provisions (even if, in the context of state action, those provisions are "incorporated" to apply against states via the Fourteenth Amendment's Due Process Clause). The other main situation where government deprives persons of life—police activity—raises difficult questions about the availability of a meaningful hearing before the government (the police officer) acts. In such cases, any due process concerns are usually accounted for by the availability of post-deprivation lawsuits. The Supreme Court has also identified the Fourth Amendment as a source of protection for victims of police violence.

Thus, "property" and "liberty" are the main concerns of procedural due process. The methodology the Court uses to define these terms has evolved significantly in the last half-century. Roughly speaking, before 1970 the Court identified property and liberty interests by asking whether the interest in question was one that had enjoyed protection under the common law, as opposed to statute. While interests protected by the common law were described as "rights," statutorily-protected interests were minimized as mere "privileges." The key point of this distinction was that, as suggested by the name, "privileges" could be revoked by government with no constitutional implications.

By the mid-twentieth century, the so-called "rights-privileges distinction" faced serious criticism. The peculiarities of the common law meant that interests that seemed intuitively similar were treated differently for purposes of the procedural protections afforded by due process. More theoretically, scholars came to question the logic of the distinction, pointing out that there was nothing about the common law that made those rights inherently more valuable or special, such that due process protected against their deprivation, as compared to rights granted by statute. In particular, scholars noted that with the rise of large-scale administrative regulation, many Americans had become deeply dependent on rights that derived from statutes. Those scholars argued that courts should begin expanding their conceptions of which interests merited due process protection as "property" or "liberty."

By the early 1970s, the Supreme Court had begun to respond. In a pair of cases from 1972, *Board of Regents v. Roth*, 408 U.S. 564 (1972), and *Perry v. Sindermann*, 408 U.S. 593 (1972), the Court set forth a new approach to identifying property and liberty interests. The Court explained that it would find such interests when the plaintiff was held to have "a legitimate claim of entitlement" to the interest. That claim would arise from some legal source—indeed, any legal source except the Due Process Clause itself. (The Due Process Clause can furnish the claim to a liberty interest in some circumstances, as explained later in this chapter.)

The Court applied this approach in *Roth* and *Perry*. Both cases dealt with claims by university professors that they had property interests in a continuation of their faculty positions at state universities. In *Roth*, the Court rejected the claim, because the professor had been hired on a one-year contract that gave him no reasonable expectation that he would be rehired. Thus, the state had given him no reason to expect that he would be able to continue in that position. By contrast, in *Perry*, the Court acknowledged the possibility that the professor in that case might have had a property interest in his job continuing. In particular, it noted that the university, even while not maintaining a formal tenure system, had distributed a faculty handbook that indicated that professors who were doing a good job and happy in their position could expect to continue to be employed. In addition, it raised the possibility that the university's normal course of dealing with faculty was to retain them for extended periods of time. Thus, even though the professor in *Perry* merely had a series of one-year contracts with the university, the Court remanded the *Perry* case to the lower court to determine whether in fact the "law" of the faculty handbook and the school's general course of dealing with faculty sufficed to give him a property interest in continued employment.

Roth and *Perry* have been influential in setting the law on the identification of liberty and property interests. Together, they stand for the proposition that the plaintiff must show that some source of law—a federal or state statute, regulation, or even something as informal as the faculty handbook at a state university—provides him with an objectively reasonable expectation that he will continue to enjoy the benefit. If he can do that, then, like the professor in *Perry* was given a chance to do when the Court remanded his case to the trial court, he can establish that he has a liberty or property interest protected by due process.

For the most part, the law that can potentially provide that interest is defined broadly, to include any state law (for Fourteenth Amendment Due Process Clause claims) and any federal law (for Fifth Amendment Due Process Clause claims). But there is one important exception to this rule. The federal Constitution (whether the Fifth or Fourteenth Amendment) does not create property interests. Such an interest can be found anywhere else in law—including anywhere else in federal law—but not in either Due Process Clause. By contrast, liberty can be found in the Due Process Clause. Recall from your Constitutional Law class that the Fifth and Fourteenth Amendments are the source of the rights you studied when you studied "substantive due process"—the (old) right to contract, the right to privacy, the right to an abortion, etc. But other than this exception, the process for finding liberty and property interests is the same, and follows the *Roth* and *Perry* template, with two final exceptions.

The first exception deals with the liberty interest one might have in one's good name—that is, the interest in not being defamed. Four years after *Roth* and *Perry*, in *Paul v. Davis*, 424 U.S. 693 (1976), the Court, without an extended discussion of those earlier cases, held that the state's deprivation of a person's interest in his good name, without more, did not trigger the procedural protections of due process. *Paul* concerned a police department's practice of publicly posting, in shopping areas, the names and photos of what the department described as "active shoplifters." The plaintiff in *Paul* found himself on that list, apparently based on a shoplifting charge that had been dismissed. Rather than suing the police department for defamation in state court, he brought a federal civil rights suit, alleging a violation of his procedural due process rights.

The Court rejected the claim, and in doing so, seemed to retreat from *Roth* and *Perry*. On the one hand, applying those cases to *Paul* would suggest that the plaintiff did indeed have a due process interest, since state law (in this case the common law) gave him a legitimate claim of expectation to the interest (since the state's common law of defamation gave him a right to recover it when that interest was impaired). The Court, however, expressed concern that that sort of analysis could convert any state law cause of action a person may have against a state government defendant into a federal due process case. The Court also cited extensive, but pre-*Roth* and *Perry*, precedent for the proposition that "the mere defamation of an individual" did not trigger the protections of due process. Instead, in the particular case of stigma, some more material harm was also needed.

In 1995, the Court cut back further on the *Roth/Perry* analysis in *Sandin v. Conner*, 515 U.S. 472 (1995). *Sandin* dealt with the due process rights of prisoners—in *Sandin*, a prisoner who was transferred to a higher-level security prison, which imposed greater restraints on his liberty. The Court held that due process only applied to such infringements if the government action imposed "atypical and significant hardship on the prisoner in relation to the ordinary incidents of prison life." Thus, a "prison manual" that gave an inmate a right to expect certain liberties does not create a due process-protected interest in those liberties unless their infringement satisfied the standard *Sandin* set forth.

Nevertheless, despite its limitations in *Paul* and *Sandin*, the Court's analysis in *Roth* and *Perry* should generally be understood as stating the modern rule for determining when an individual possesses an interest protected by due process. A couple of examples illustrate how the analysis works. In *Goss v. Lopez*, 419 U.S. 565 (1975), the Court held that a public school student had a due process-protected interest in remaining in school, despite a misconduct charge, because of a state law that gave all students the right to a public education. Similarly, in *Barry v. Barchi*, 443 U.S. 55 (1979), a horse trainer was held to have a due process right to his trainer license in light of a state law that entitled a licensed trainer to keep his license unless he was shown to have engaged in misconduct. These straightforward examples illustrate both how the *Roth* and *Perry* analysis works, and its continued force despite *Paul* and *Sandin*.

B. What Constitutes a Deprivation?

As with the existence of a due process-protected interest, the question of when an individual has been deprived of such an interest has some intuitive applications, but also some not so intuitive ones. Certainly, it is the case that an intentional decision by government, made in the normal course of business, that a person no longer merits a benefit—say, a government job—constitutes a deprivation of that interest. But in two other situations courts have held that there has been no deprivation, even though the plaintiff has lost property or liberty.

First, if the deprivation happened accidentally, then there will be no "deprivation" for purposes of the Due Process Clause. This limitation makes a great deal of sense when one assumes, as the law does, that the point of the Due Process Clause is to give the affected person a right to a hearing when an important interest is at stake. It would make little sense to say that, for example, the federal government had to provide a hearing before a postal service truck collided with your car and thus damaged your property. To be sure, you might have a right to a post-deprivation remedy (a tort suit against the postal service), but as a general matter it doesn't make much conceptual sense to speak of these cases as implicating the due process right to a hearing. For example, in *Daniels v. Williams*, 474 U.S. 327 (1986), a prisoner was held not to have suffered a deprivation of a due process-protected interest when he slipped and fell on a pillow that was negligently left on a staircase.

Second, and perhaps less intuitively, if the government agent in question was acting beyond the scope of his governmentally-granted authority, then again that will not constitute a case where the government has "deprived" the individual of his property or liberty. For example, if a prison guard goes on a private vendetta against an inmate and destroys the inmate's property, due process will not be implicated. *See Hudson v. Palmer*, 468 U.S. 517 (1984). The Court in *Hudson* explained that, just as with negligent deprivations, a pre-deprivation hearing in this latter context is simply impracticable. Note, however, that the *Hudson* Court conditioned this holding on the existence of a *post*-deprivation remedy, such as a tort suit. It is thus possible to read *Hudson* as speaking to question 3 (how much process is due)—in this case, concluding that such a post-deprivation remedy is all the process that is constitutionally required, given the impracticality of a pre-deprivation hearing.

C. How Much Process Is Due?

Assume that both questions addressed up to now are answered in the affirmative: the interest in question does count as a due process-protected right, and the government has in fact deprived the individual of that right. How much process is constitutionally required in order for that deprivation to be constitutional, as "due process"?

In the early part of the twentieth century, the Court commented, rather casually, that due process necessarily included the right to make an oral presentation, even if that presentation was informal. *See Londoner v. Denver*, 210 U.S. 373 (1908). (Recall that *Londoner* is discussed in more detail in Chapter 5.) However, by the mid-1970s, it was clear that the amount of process that was constitutionally due had to be more carefully tailored to the situation. Recall that during that era the Court was expanding the scope of interests protected by the Due Process Clause (*i.e.*, it was providing a more expansive answer to the first of the three questions presented in this chapter). With that expansion came a realization that a pre-deprivation oral hearing did not always make sense. For example, such a hearing might add significant costs to the government, especially since more "mass justice" programs, such as disability, Social Security, and welfare benefits were now being considered due process-protected interests, rather than mere statutory "privileges." It was also thought that eligibility for at least some of these benefits was relatively easy to determine with something less than an oral hearing. Further complicating this situation was the reality that many agencies in fact provided an opportunity for an oral hearing, but only after the benefits in question had been cut off. Thus, in many cases the claim came down to a timing issue—that is, an issue not *whether*, but *when*, an oral hearing had to be provided in order to satisfy due process.

One thing the Court has *not* done is to import the *Roth/Perry* expectations approach into the context of this third question. In *Arnett v. Kennedy*, 416 U.S. 134 (1974), a plurality of the Court attempted to do so. Essentially, the plurality in *Arnett* explained that, if law-based expectations determine the existence of a due process protected interest in the first place, then they should also determine the constitutionality of the amount of the process the government offered when it withdrew that benefit. Thus, on this theory, if a state law gave a state employee an expectation that he could continue to stay in his job, but if that same law provided a very paltry appeals process if the state decided he no longer qualified, then both sets of expectations—of the interest but also of the process he was due—would be honored by courts. The plurality called this idea "the bitter with the sweet," on the theory that the individual would have to take the "bitter" (the paltry process the statute offered him) if he wanted to claim the "sweet" (the property interest that same statute offered him). A majority of the Court rejected this idea, and instead insisted that the third question—how much process was due—had to be decided by courts, without any reference to any expectations the state might have given the claimant.

The result of all this thinking was *Mathews v. Eldridge*, 424 U.S. 319 (1976), which distilled the evolving law of how much process was constitutionally due into a three-factor test. *Mathews* dealt with a decision by the Social Security Administration that a recipient of Social Security disability benefits was no longer disabled, and thus no longer qualified for those benefits. The agency offered the individual a chance to dispute the agency's conclusion before the benefits were cut off, but only in writing (for example, in the form of a doctor's report about the recipient's medical condition). But, as alluded to two paragraphs above, the agency also offered the opportunity of an oral hearing, but only after the benefits had terminated. In determining how much process the agency had to provide persons who fell into that category—in particular, whether it had to offer a pre-deprivation oral hearing— the Court adopted a three-pronged balancing test.

First, the Court considered the importance of the interest to the class of recipients. Note that this is *not* a question of how important the benefit—say, the disability check—was to that particular recipient who was suing. Realize that that approach would mean that each and every recipient of a benefit could claim a constitutional right to additional process, based on the importance of the benefit in question to that particular recipient. That type of system, in which the amount of process that was constitutionally due shifted with each recipient and had to be litigated with each recipient, would clearly be unworkable. Thus, the Court held that this first prong had to be analyzed with respect to the class as a whole—in *Mathews*, for example, the class of Social Security disability benefit recipients.

Second, the Court considered the degree to which the agency's current procedures produced accurate results, and the improvement in accuracy, if any, that could be expected if the agency were required to provide the procedures requested by the plaintiff. Thus, in *Mathews*, when the plaintiff requested an oral hearing prior to the cut-off of his disability checks, the Court had to consider the extent to which the written process the agency allowed before the benefit cut-off produced generally accurate eligibility decisions, and the degree to which an oral hearing would increase that accuracy.

Third, the Court considered the government interests at stake. In *Mathews*, the Court noted that a requirement of a pre-benefit-termination oral hearing would likely lead to many more requests for such hearings as compared with the current system, which allowed such hearings only after benefits were no longer flowing to the individual. This would require the hiring of more claim adjudicators. In addition, it would cost the agency more in terms of benefits paid out, since a claimant would have every incentive to exercise the oral hearing right, even if he knew he was going to lose, since the benefits would continue to flow during the pendency of that oral hearing process. (To be sure, in *Mathews* the agency's procedures provided for recapturing benefits found to have been paid out in error, but the Court was skeptical that the agency would succeed at clawing back much of that money, given the general neediness and lack of resources of persons receiving disability checks.)

Before considering how the *Mathews* Court applied these factors, think about them for a moment. One might be tempted to think about these factors as inputs into a mathematical equation. On this reading, if the importance of the right to the class of recipients (Factor 1), multiplied by the increased accuracy that one could expect from the requested additional procedures (Factor 2), exceeded the cost to the government in providing those procedures (Factor 3) then the Constitution would be held to require them. An opposite result would lead to the opposite legal conclusion. The Court, however, warned readers away from this approach, explaining that these three factors are simply considerations courts had to think about when performing the due process analysis.

This warning makes sense, given the difficulty in quantifying these factors, and thus the difficulty of translating them into the inputs of an equation. Consider Factor 1. All the *Mathews* Court could say about the importance of disability checks to the class of recipients is that that importance was relatively less than the importance of welfare checks to that class of those recipients, given that welfare was expressly designed for individuals who otherwise would have no way to support themselves. (The Court had decided a case dealing with welfare cut-off procedures, *Goldberg v. Kelly*, 397 U.S. 254 (1970), several years before.) By contrast, even a wealthy worker who became disabled was eligible for a disability check. Nevertheless, the Court acknowledged that, as a general matter, recipients of disability checks did not have many resources. One can easily understand how this very vague quantification of this factor would make it difficult to see the overall *Mathews* test as a rigid, quantifiable equation.

The Court was more confident about Factor 2. It noted that disability determinations were professional medical determinations. It thus observed that the most pertinent information about those determinations came from written documents, such as doctor's reports, x-rays, test results and the like. For that reason, it doubted that an opportunity for oral presentation would add much to what it speculated was already a highly accurate eligibility determination process. It again contrasted this situation to one it had confronted several years before in *Goldberg*, on the theory that welfare eligibility turned on criteria (such as whether the recipient was living with someone who had resources) that could be best uncovered by oral testimony from the recipient himself and those who came in contact with him, such as neighbors.

Coming to Factor 3, the Court observed that eligibility for a pre-termination oral hearing would likely cost the government a not-insignificant sum, given the resulting need to hire more claim adjudicators, especially since invoking the hearing option would then allow a claimant to keep receiving benefits until the hearing took place. In addition to the cost of hiring those adjudicators, the Court also suggested that it would also have to pay out more in benefits, with little hope of recouping payments erroneously made, given most recipients' lack of resources to pay any governmental claim.

Weighing these factors, the Court concluded that the high accuracy of the current procedures, when combined with the specter of increased governmental costs if pre-termination oral hearings were required, justified the agency's practice of making eligibility decisions based on a paper record, with oral hearings allowed only after the benefits were cut off.

Despite the relative straightforwardness of this application of the *Mathews* factors, at times the Court has suggested more expansive approaches to those factors. For example, in *Board of Curators of the University of Missouri v. Horowitz*, 435 U.S. 78 (1978), the Court rejected a claim that due process required an adversarial-type hearing before a medical student was academically disqualified from her program. The Court explained that the mentoring role of a faculty member in making academic decisions counseled against adversarializing the process by which such decisions were made. Similarly, in *Walters v. National Association of Radiation Survivors*, 473 U.S. 305 (1985), the Court upheld a congressional scheme for the compensation of service members exposed to radiation, even though that scheme severely limited the ability of claimants to pay more than a nominal amount for an attorney to represent them, and thus limited the practical ability of claimants to bring a lawyer into the process. As in *Horowitz*, the Court insisted that adversarializing the process, here by allowing claimants an easier time to bring a lawyer into the room, might work to their detriment, as the government case worker on the other side of the table might feel less inclined to assist the claimant in that case, and might instead be more inclined to adopt an adversarial posture herself. These cases, while in some ways speaking to *Mathews* Factor 2, suggest how the Court has employed that factor in flexible ways.

Consider also *Cleveland Board of Education v. Loudermill*, 470 U.S. 532 (1985), in which the Court expressed a similarly expansive understanding of Factor 2, but this time in favor of requiring *more* process. *Loudermill* involved a state decision that a state employee had lied on his job application when he asserted that had never been convicted of a felony. In one sense, the state's decision was absolutely accurate based on the paper record—in a real way, all it had to do was compare two sheets of paper, the employee's job application and his conviction record, to conclude that, in fact, he had lied. But the employee insisted that he had a right to tell his side of the story, and to explain that in fact he had thought the conviction in question was a misdemeanor. The Court held that Factor 2 cut in favor of the employee. It concluded that the government's interest in accurate decision making in this case militated in favor of hearing the employee out, so the state could make not just a formally accurate opinion, but one that was properly informed by the equities of the situation.

Loudermill also introduced the possibility of a more expansive reading of Factor 3. Recall from *Mathews* that the Court understood Factor 3 as focused on the government's interest in avoiding the cost of both additional adjudicators and added benefits payouts. In *Loudermill*, the Court understood Factor 3 as also including the government's interest in not firing an employee who deserved to stay on the job. Thus, the government's interest included an interest in *more* process—the same interest the plaintiff himself had. This example should drive the point home that you should not understand the *Mathews* factors as inputs into an equation: in this case, the claimant's and government's interest would be on the same side of any such equation.

These examples make it clear that *Mathews* has to be applied in a nuanced, non-rigid way. Indeed, sometimes the Court doesn't even apply *Mathews* to due process issues. For example, in *Dusenbery v. United States*, 534 U.S. 161 (2002), a prison inmate had had some of his property seized as part of the investigation that led to his conviction. The government ultimately sold the property off as being forfeited, after placing notices in several newspapers. The inmate sued, alleging that the notice of the impending forfeiture failed the requirements of due process. The Court agreed, but, more importantly for our purposes, it declined to apply *Mathews* but instead applied a simpler, pre-*Mathews* test governing the adequacy of notice in similar situations.

Thus, while it's certainly a critical precedent for question 3 of the due process inquiry, you should not immediately assume that a court will apply *Mathews* to a particular case. And when it does, these final cases show that the application of *Mathews* may well be nuanced and sometimes surprising.

D. The Problem of Bias and *Ex Parte* Contacts

As you might guess, due process requires an impartial decisionmaker. This requirement raises the issue of biased decision makers, and, somewhat relatedly, the problem *ex parte* contacts cause for the concept of a fundamentally fair process. These issues are taken up in the next chapter.

The short version: Interests protected by due process are generally those to which an individual has an objectively reasonable expectation, with that expectation flowing from some source of law other than the federal Constitution. The only exception to this rule is that liberty interests, in addition to being findable in that way, can also be found in the Due Process Clause itself. For purposes of the Due Process Clause, a "deprivation" must be an intentional action by government made in the normal course of its conduct, rather than, say, an unintended action caused by negligence. If an interest is protected by due process, then courts will usually determine how much process is constitutionally required by balancing (1) the importance of the interest to the class of recipients, (2) the increased accuracy that could be expected from applying the procedures the plaintiff demands, and (3) the government's interest.

Ex Parte Contacts and
Bias in Adjudication

This chapter examines the same integrity issues Chapter 8 examined, but this time in the context of adjudication. As with that earlier chapter, this one begins by discussing *ex parte* contacts. It then examines the problem of decision-makers—in this chapter, adjudicators—who are alleged to have been biased, or to have made up their minds before the adjudicative process itself. As you'll see, the rules Chapter 8 discussed in the context of rulemaking integrity have some applicability here as well. However, adjudicative integrity is also governed by other rules.

A. *Ex Parte* Contacts in Adjudication

The APA does not have any provisions restricting *ex parte* contacts in informal adjudication. Of course, due process might impose some restrictions, since such contacts conflict with the very idea of a fundamentally fair hearing. Nevertheless, the law in this area is unclear, in part because no clear answers to questions like these arise from the *Mathews v. Eldridge* due process balancing test explained in the prior chapter. Still, courts have recognized that *ex parte* contacts have the potential to violate due process. *See, e.g.,* *United States Lines v. Federal Maritime Commission,* 584 F.2d 519, 539 (D.C. Cir. 1978) ("The inconsistency of secret *Ex parte* contacts with the notion of a fair hearing and with the principles of fairness implicit in due process has long been recognized.").

By contrast, the APA imposes significant limitations on *ex parte* contacts in *formal* adjudication. Chapter 8 considered integrity issues in the context of rulemaking. Recall that that chapter explained that Section 557(d) restricts *external ex parte* contacts (that is, *ex parte* contacts between the agency presiding official and interested persons *outside* the agency). That section of the APA applies to both formal rulemaking and formal adjudication. You should review that chapter when you study the limits on *ex parte* contacts in formal adjudication.

But formal adjudication is governed by an additional set of limits on *ex parte* contacts, those that might occur *within* an agency. For example, an ALJ conducting a formal adjudication may decide, after formally closing the hearing and retiring to his office to decide the case, that he needs additional information that he could obtain from an expert within the agency. Such a communication would not be governed by Section 557(d), but it is covered by Section 554(d).

For our purposes, section 554(d) can be understood as essentially four parts. The first two parts read as follows:

"Except to the extent required for the disposition of ex parte matters as authorized by law, [the person who presides over the presentation of the evidence in an adjudication] may not—

(1)   consult a person or party on a fact in issue, unless on notice and opportunity for all parties to participate; or

(2)   be responsible to or subject to the supervision or direction of an employee or agent engaged in the performance of investigative or prosecuting functions for an agency."

These are straightforward provisions, although the first one is not free of ambiguity. The first prevents the ALJ from speaking with "a person or party on a fact in issue" unless she formally re-opens the hearing, and gives all parties notice and a chance to participate. Thus, in the prototypical example described above, the ALJ could not simply walk down the hall at the agency and speak to an agency expert about "a fact in issue" in the case. Instead, the ALJ could only do so as part of the formal adjudicative process over which she is presiding.

Still, a degree of ambiguity lurks in this provision. For example, presumably the ALJ should be able to consult a law clerk or administrative assistant about "a fact in issue"—for example, by asking his law clerk her opinion about a factual question in the case or asking the assistant for help in locating files relevant to such a fact. Probably the best reading of this provision is that the office of the ALJ should be understood as a unit, such that this type of consultation would not run afoul of this section. There should probably be even less of a problem if the ALJ pulls off his shelf a book written by an agency employee that is relevant to such a fact, despite the argument that, in effect, he would be "consult[ing]" the author of the work on that fact. Despite these common-sense observations, the relative sparseness of the case law leaves these questions not formally and conclusively resolved.

The second of these provisions is more straightforward. It seeks to ensure that ALJs are not subject to the supervision of investigators or prosecutors, and thus subject to pressures to please or be responsive to their desires (presumably, for decisions favorable to the prosecutions brought by the agency). This results in a bureaucratic structure at most agencies in which the adjudicative function is at least somewhat walled off from the departments responsible for investigating and prosecuting. Note that this restriction prevents ALJs from being subject to the control of "an employee or agent" engaged in prosecutions or investigations. Thus, the agency head remains able to supervise ALJs, at least indirectly, even if the agency head is understood as performing investigative or prosecutorial functions. This makes sense, given that most federal agencies include the adjudicative function, and thus that ALJs would have to be subject to supervision by the agency head. (In some states ALJs are completely separated from the agencies over which they have adjudicative responsibility.)

The third provision shifts focus, from the ALJ to others in the agency. It reads as follows:

> "An employee or agent engaged in the performance of investigative or prosecuting functions for an agency in a case may not, in that or a factually related case, participate or advise in the decision, recommended decision, or agency review pursuant to section 557 of this title, except as witness or counsel in public proceedings."

We'll talk about this provision in the context of the fourth and final provision. That fourth provision reads, in relevant part, as follows:

> "This subsection does not apply— . . .
>
> (C) to the agency or a member or members of the body comprising the agency."

Recall that an agency head can often act as an appellate institution, reviewing the decisions of ALJs. This final provision makes the restrictions on ALJs inapplicable to agency heads. Thus, for example, the agency head, unlike the ALJ, can engage in the proverbial walk down the hall noted earlier, to discuss a fact in a case with an agency expert. It makes sense to allow the agency head to have this discretion. After all, the expert down the hall is part of the agency's apparatus, which the agency head controls. It might seem odd to restrict the agency head from the ability to speak with that expert. The good sense here only becomes clearer when one realizes that agency heads are usually political appointees, who may not have a built-in store of knowledge about the technical matters facing the agency. Thus, it may be appropriate to allow them to consult agency experts informally.

But wait. The third provision does not limit the discretion of the adjudicator (whether the ALJ or the agency head); instead, it speaks to prosecutors and witnesses. Thus, the leeway the agency head enjoys to consult agency personnel on facts related to a pending case does not authorize her to have *ex parte* conversations with witnesses and prosecutors. To be sure, that third provision does not limit the agency head; as the fourth provision makes clear, nothing in Section 554(d) limits that person. However, it does limit "[a]n employee or agent engaged in the performance of investigative or prosecuting functions for an agency." Thus, while the agency head might be able to ask such a person about a fact relevant to the case on which the prosecutor or witness was working (or a factually-related one), the prosecutor or witness would not be allowed to answer.

This restriction, which, again, restricts even an agency head's practical ability to communicate with some persons in her agency, reflects the concern with the integrity of the formal process to which Section 554 applies. It may be one thing to allow the agency head/adjudicator to speak with experts down the hall, but if those experts were playing a particular role in that formal process—that is, if they served as either witnesses or prosecutors—then even the agency head is limited in her ability to speak with them *ex parte*. This careful balancing of the practicalities of agencies' structures with the need for procedural regularity reflects the larger balancing between, on the one hand, those practicalities, and, on the other, the need to ensure the integrity of the most formalized of agency procedures, formal adjudication.

B. Bias and Prejudgment in Adjudication

Bias and prejudgment in adjudication arise when an agency official has either actually or given the appearance of having made up her mind about an issue before the subject of the adjudication has had a chance to speak. The unfairness of such a process is, of course, obvious; indeed, it renders that process a sham, to the extent the agency official has already effectively decided the case.

One context in which this issue has arisen is when an agency plays different roles. For example, in *Withrow v. Larkin*, 421 U.S. 35 (1975), a state medical agency was accused of having violated the Fourteenth Amendment due process rights of a doctor who was the target of administrative investigation and adjudicative proceedings. The doctor/plaintiff alleged that due process was necessarily violated when the same agency both performed the preliminary investigation that caused the adjudication to be pursued, and also presided over the ensuing adjudication. The theory, of course, was that the initial decision that there was sufficient evidence to proceed to a hearing had biased the agency in favor of a finding that, indeed, the doctor was guilty of the charges alleged. The doctor thus argued that due process was violated whenever an agency combined investigatory, prosecutorial, and adjudicative functions.

The Court rejected that argument. It conceded that the problem was real, but it held that the plaintiff's argument—that due process was violated whenever such a combination of functions existed—was far too broad. The Court noted that courts often heard cases about which they had previously made decisions without any inherent violation of due process, for example, when a court concluded that there was probable cause to arrest someone and then presided over the eventual trial. Thus, the Court concluded that, in most cases, whether or not there was a due process violation would have to turn on the particular facts of the case.

Before turning to examples of such particular fact patterns, note that *Withrow* acknowledged two situations in which the reality or the appearance of impartiality was necessarily called into question, and which required that a different decision-maker hear the case. The first was when the decision-maker had a pecuniary interest in the outcome of the case. The leading case on this point is *Tumey v. Ohio*, 273 U.S. 510 (1925). In *Tumey*, the adjudicator in a local court received a component of his compensation only if the defendant was found guilty. The Court had no difficulty concluding that the adjudicator's pecuniary interest in a particular outcome created the reality or the appearance of bias in a way that violated due process. The second situation involves cases where the adjudicator is the subject of personal abuse from one of the parties. The Court in *Withrow* observed that human nature suggested that that adjudicator could not be expected to remain unbiased, or at least could not be perceived as remaining unbiased, if he was the victim of such abuse. Other than these two situations, however, the question of when due process is violated by the reality or appearance of bias or prejudgment has to turn on the facts.

In deciding these cases, courts have focused on the types of facts that have been alleged to be prejudged. If the facts allegedly being prejudged are "legislative," "policy," or "social" facts—that is, facts about the world generally, rather than about the particular subject of the adjudication—then any alleged prejudgment is hard to challenge. In such a case the plaintiff has to show that the agency adjudicator had an "irrevocably closed mind." For example, in *FTC v. Cement Institute*, 333 U.S. 683 (1948), cement manufacturers accused by the agency of illegal pricing practices complained that the agency had prejudged the issue because commissioners of the agency had earlier stated to Congress that they believed that those practices did indeed violate the law, in the context of a different industry. The Court rejected the challenge, remarking that to rule otherwise would defeat Congress's purpose in creating an agency that would both inform Congress about industry conditions and adjudicate violations of federal fair-trade laws. It also noted that the parties had ample opportunity to provide information during the adjudication in an attempt to convince the agency that their practices were legal.

By contrast, courts have taken a more plaintiff-friendly approach when considering claims that the adjudicator has prejudged facts particular to the defendant. The two leading cases here both deal with the same agency, and, indeed, the same agency head. In *Cinderella Finishing Schools v. Federal Trade Commission*, 425 F.2d 583 (D.C. Cir. 1970), a commissioner of the FTC made a speech that seemed to speak to the precise factual allegations made against a party in an FTC adjudication which was pending in front of the commission (including this particular commissioner). The court held that this violated the rule that asked "whether a disinterested observer may conclude that the agency has in some measure adjudged the facts as well as the law of a particular case in advance of hearing it." Several years earlier the court had decided a similar case, involving the exact same FTC commissioner, applying the same test, and again finding a violation of due process. *Texaco, Inc. v. FTC*, 336 F.2d 754 (D.C. Cir. 1964). The table at the end of this chapter calls this the "*Cinderella* Standard."

Why this more lenient standard in these latter cases? It's tempting to focus on the oddity that both cases involved what might have been an overly-aggressive (and not particularly due process-sensitive) agency head. But there's a larger reality to the distinction between *Cinderella* and *Texaco* on the one hand, and *Cement Institute* on the other.

First, when an agency prejudges facts about the particular party, it likely deprives itself of input from the best source of information about such facts—the party itself. Thus, if accuracy means anything to the due process calculus—and recall the second *Mathews v. Eldridge* factor from the previous chapter, which focuses exactly on accuracy—then one might be especially concerned by prejudgment of these particularized facts. By contrast, one might not be so concerned if the agency has strong pre-existing views about broader policy facts, such as the question whether the pricing practice at issue in *Cement Institute* violated federal fair-trade laws. The parties might well have good information on that question, but there's no reason to think the agency itself would lack access to information that's just as good. Thus, accuracy is not as seriously undermined if these broader types of facts are prejudged.

Second, as the *Cement Institute* Court implied, agencies could not exist as currently constituted if they were forbidden from learning the broader policy facts about their particular regulatory areas and at the same time adjudicating claims against particular parties under their organic statutes. As long as the agency had not conclusively prejudged the issue—that is, as long as it did not have an "irrevocably closed mind," it could have opinions on these issues and still adjudicate these claims, since this standard requires only that the agency be open to having its mind changed as a result of the party's factual or legal presentation.

Note a parallel here. The "irrevocably closed mind" standard from *Cement Institute* is, for all practical purposes, the equivalent of the "unalterably closed mind" standard from the *National Advertisers* case that was discussed in the context of bias and prejudgment in *rulemaking*. (That case, and that material, is presented in Chapter 8(B).) Why the parallel? Because in both situations the facts that were prejudged—in *National Advertisers* the misleading nature of children's advertising, and in *Cement Institute* the legality of a particular pricing practice—constitute "social," "policy," or "legislative" facts. In both cases we'd naturally expect the agencies to have pre-existing views on these issues. In both cases the agency could not operate as designed if it was forbidden from having such pre-existing views. And in both cases, there's less of a concern about agency conclusions being wrong because they already had opinions about the issues in question. Thus, in a fundamental way, the bias and prejudgment question turns less on the format of the agency proceeding (rulemaking versus adjudication) and more on the nature of the facts that were allegedly prejudged ("social," "policy," or "legislative" versus particularized or "adjudicative").

Let's now put together the rule from *National Advertisers* and the cases discussed in this chapter, to get an overall sense of the legal standards applied to various claims of bias and prejudgment.

Table 2: The Standards Governing Claims of
Unconstitutional Bias or Prejudgment

	Rulemaking	Adjudication
Adjudicative Facts		"*Cinderella* Standard" (more plaintiff-friendly)
Policy/Legislative Facts	"Unalterably/ Irrevocably Closed Mind" Standard (*National Advertisers*)	"Unalterably/ Irrevocably Closed Mind" Standard (*Cement Institute*)

This chart illustrates how the relevant tests for bias and prejudgment turn not on whether the agency is engaged in rulemaking or adjudication, but rather on the type of facts allegedly being prejudged. Note that the upper left-hand box is empty. That's for a reason: it would be highly unusual for an agency to have to find—let alone to have the opportunity to prejudge—adjudicative facts (that is, facts about a particular party) in the course of doing a rulemaking. To repeat what we discussed in Chapter 5, that's because rulemaking focuses on broad social facts, rather than facts about any particular party.

The short version: The APA does not impose limits on *ex parte* contacts in informal adjudication, but the Due Process Clause imposes some vaguely-defined limits. However, in the context of formal adjudication the APA does impose significant limits on both external *ex parte* contacts (Section 557(d)) and *ex parte* contacts among agency personnel (Section 554(d)). The Due Process Clause also imposes limits on an adjudicator's pre-judgment of facts that are the subject of the litigation, with those limits turning on whether the facts being prejudged are particularized to the individual litigant or, by contrast, are more general social or policy facts. These limits are more stringent when the adjudicator pre-judges particularized facts about the individual litigant.

* * * * *

THE TAKEAWAY

What are the main issues this Part addresses?

- **The legal source of the procedural rules governing agency adjudication.**

    Informal agency adjudication is governed, for the most part, by the Due Process Clause, with APA Sections 555 and 706 imposing minimal procedural requirements on agencies. Formal agency adjudication is governed by APA Sections 554,

556, and 557, which impose trial-type procedures on agency adjudications.

- **The agency's discretion to choose between formal and informal adjudication.**

  Lower courts are split on whether the presumption of informality that governs rulemaking also applies in adjudication. In addition, some courts will defer to the agency's choice to employ informal procedures if the organic statute is ambiguous on that question.

- **When the Due Process Clause applies to an agency adjudication.**

  In order for the Due Process Clause to apply to a particular adjudication, the interest at stake has to be one in which the individual holds an objectively reasonable expectation, based on some legal source, in the continuation of that benefit.

- **The procedures that are constitutionally required by the Due Process Clause.**

  Usually, a court will answer this question by applying the three factors from *Mathews v. Eldridge*: (1) the importance of the interest to the class of recipients, (2) the increased accuracy that could be expected if the agency is required to employ the procedures the plaintiff demands, and (3) the government's interest.

- **The integrity rules that apply to adjudications.**

  Formal agency adjudication is governed by Section 557(d)'s limits on external *ex parte* contacts and Section 554(d)'s limits on internal *ex parte* contacts. Informal agency adjudication is not subject to any APA-based *ex parte* communications requirements. Bias or prejudgment of facts is a matter of concern for purposes of fundamental fairness under the Due

Process Clause, as applied both to formal and informal agency adjudication.

PART FOUR

The Availability of
Judicial Review

Judicial review is a crucial part of administrative law. The legitimacy of agency action turns to a large degree on the fact that a federal court is always available to review whether the agency has followed the appropriate procedures, correctly found the facts and interpreted its organic statute, and made reasonable policy decisions. Thus, a critical part of administrative law consists of determining whether and on what conditions a plaintiff may seek judicial review of an agency's action.

This Part of the *Guide* considers these issues. After the following introductory chapter, Chapter 16 considers whether such review is available at all. Chapter 17 then discusses the parties to the action, both by explaining when a plaintiff has standing to sue an agency and how the doctrine of sovereign immunity impacts the ability to sue an agency. Chapter 18 discusses what form that sort of lawsuit can take, and issues surrounding federal court jurisdiction. Finally, Chapter 19 explains the doctrines governing the timing of such suits.

The sequence of these parts tracks how the APA deals with them, in Chapter 7 of that statute. Thus, this Part of the *Guide* begins with a quick walk-through of that part of the APA, to explain its architecture and to note how it deals, in sequence, with each of the issues discussed in the previous paragraph.

CHAPTER 15

The APA and the Availability of Judicial Review

Chapter 7 of the APA, 5 U.S.C. §§ 701-706, deals with judicial review. Section 706 considers the powers courts have once they reach the merits of a case challenging agency action. For that reason, we will defer consideration of that section until Part Five of this *Guide*. But the other sections are relevant to the availability of judicial review. Because it's important to understand how these provisions build on each other to create a coherent picture of the availability of judicial review under the APA, this chapter provides a very quick overview of Sections 701 through 705. Each of the topics discussed here will be treated in more detail in subsequent chapters. For now, just try to get a sense of how the APA proceeds methodically to set forth a plaintiff's ability to seek judicial review.

A. Section 701

Section 701 sets forth when the rest of Chapter 7 of the APA applies. For purposes of that chapter, it defines "agency" broadly, to include the institutions what we ordinarily think about when we think about "agencies," such as the Environmental Protection Agency, the Securities and Exchange Commission, and other similar entities. For those "agencies," Section 701 has been understood to establish what the Supreme Court has called "the presumption of reviewability"—that is, the presumption that the actions of such agencies are subject to judicial review. This presumption is not explicitly stated in Section 701, however. The relevant section of Section 701 states as follows:

> "(a) This chapter applies, according to the provisions thereof, except to the extent that—
>
> (1)   statutes preclude judicial review; or
>
> (2)   agency action is committed to agency discretion by law."

Thus, this provision states that "[t]his chapter" (*i.e.*, Chapter 7 of the APA, dealing with judicial review) applies, unless one of the two stated exceptions exists. As we'll see in Chapter 16, these exceptions tend to be read narrowly, thus making most agency action subject to judicial review.

B.   Section 702

Section 702 deals with the parties to a lawsuit challenging agency action. It reads in relevant part as follows:

> "A person suffering legal wrong because of agency action, or adversely affected or aggrieved by agency action within the meaning of a relevant statute, is entitled to judicial review thereof. An action in a court of the United States seeking relief other than money damages and stating a claim that an agency or an officer or employee thereof acted or failed to act in an official capacity or under color of legal authority shall not be dismissed nor relief therein be denied on the ground that it is against

the United States or that the United States is an indispensable party. The United States may be named as a defendant in any such action, and a judgment or decree may be entered against the United States . . . ."

The first sentence states who is allowed to be plaintiff—that is, who has standing—in a lawsuit challenging agency action. As you may recall from other classes, standing is governed in part by the Constitution's requirement that there be an actual "case or controversy." Such constitutional, or "Article III" standing applies to lawsuits challenging agency action just like to any other federal court lawsuit. Chapter 17 will discuss Article III standing. But that chapter will also discuss what the first sentence of Section 702 means for plaintiffs' attempts to sue agencies. As we will see, that sentence has been interpreted as requiring that the plaintiff, in addition to having Article III standing, also be "arguably within the zone of interests sought to be protected by the [organic] statute."

The second sentence of Section 702 deals with the government-defendant. For our purposes, it waives federal sovereign immunity to the extent the lawsuit does not seek damages. Thus, it allows lawsuits in which the plaintiff requests, for example, a declaratory judgment or, even more relevantly to administrative law, an injunction against the agency taking a particular action (for example, enforcing a regulation that the court finds illegal). As you can imagine, these are important types of cases in administrative law, as they seek to restrain an agency from taking a given action.

C. Section 703

Section 703 is important for what it says but also for what it does not say. It reads as follows:

"The form of proceeding for judicial review is the special statutory review proceeding relevant to the subject matter in a court specified by statute or, in the absence or inadequacy thereof, any applicable form of legal action, including actions for declaratory judgments or writs of prohibitory or mandatory injunction or habeas corpus, in a court of competent jurisdiction. If no special statutory review proceeding is applicable, the action for judicial review may be brought against the United States, the agency by its official title, or the appropriate officer. Except to the extent that prior, adequate, and exclusive opportunity for judicial review is provided by law, agency action is subject to judicial review in civil or criminal proceedings for judicial enforcement."

Section 703 speaks to what the lawsuit should look like—that is, what type of action, *e.g.*, a petition for a writ of habeas corpus, is the appropriate one. Essentially, Section 703 directs you to the agency's organic statute: if that statute specifies the type of action that can be employed to challenge the agency's action, then that is what is allowed, unless that type of action is inadequate (for example, by providing inadequate relief). In that latter case, Section 703 is very generous about allowing any other appropriate form of action, such as, for example, an action for a declaratory judgment or a writ of habeas corpus. (One might imagine a plaintiff seeking a writ of habeas corpus if, for example, the agency in question is the Office of Immigration and Customs Enforcement (ICE), which has taken someone into custody.) When the organic statute does not provide a particular review proceeding, or when that proceeding is inadequate, Section 703 specifies who can be named as the defendant in that more generally-authorized lawsuit. Finally, Section 703 makes clear that unless some earlier opportunity was provided to challenge the agency action in question, it can be challenged when an agency seeks to enforce that action against a person.

But there's one important thing Section 703 does *not* do. Note that it authorizes more generally-applicable lawsuits "in a court of competent jurisdiction." Neither Section 703 nor any other APA provision provides a federal court with jurisdiction. Chapter 18, in addition to setting forth details about what's discussed above, also explains where a court can find federal court jurisdiction to challenge agency action.

D. Section 704

Section 704 addresses the timing of judicial review—that is, when a lawsuit can be brought and decided. It states as follows:

> "Agency action made reviewable by statute and final agency action for which there is no other adequate remedy in a court are subject to judicial review. A preliminary, procedural, or intermediate agency action or ruling not directly reviewable is subject to review on the review of the final agency action. Except as otherwise expressly required by statute, agency action otherwise final is final for the purposes of this section whether or not there has been presented or determined an application for a declaratory order, for any form of reconsideration, or, unless the agency otherwise requires by rule and provides that the action meanwhile is inoperative, for an appeal to superior agency authority."

Section 704 does several things relevant to timing. The first sentence explains that if the relevant organic statute makes an action reviewable, then that action is indeed subject to judicial review. Thus, for example, if the organic statute specifies that an otherwise-preliminary sounding action is nevertheless subject to judicial review then it is reviewable, subject to constitutional constraints noted in the next paragraph. It then says, importantly, that in addition, "final agency action for which there is no other adequate remedy in a court" is also subject to judicial review. As we'll see, "finality" is an important timing concept when a plaintiff seeks judicial review of an agency action. The second sentence makes clear that preliminary agency decisions that may not be immediately reviewable can be reviewed when the agency takes a final action. Finally, the long, convoluted last sentence of Section 704 speaks to when a would-be plaintiff has to exhaust her remedies within the agency before seeking review in front of an Article III court. "Exhaustion" is another important timing concept. All these concepts will be discussed in Chapter 19.

There is yet another important timing issue that Chapter 19 will discuss. In addition to "finality" and "exhaustion," courts also have to satisfy themselves that a challenge to agency action is "ripe." Ripeness is a judge-made doctrine that, as you might guess from the name, speaks to when the case in question is "ripe"—that is, when it's ready for a court to decide. As we'll see in Chapter 19(A), ripeness doctrine is a mixture of Article III concerns—that is, concerns about whether the lawsuit presents a "case or controversy"—and so-called "prudential" concerns—that is, concerns that speak more to good judicial common sense than to constitutional concerns. For now, the important thing to note is that even though an action may be final, and even though there may be no need for the plaintiff to exhaust her agency remedies, a court may still decide that the issue isn't ripe. Indeed, to the extent a decision about non-ripeness is based on constitutional concerns, Congress is not able to override that decision, say, by specifying in the organic statute that a particular agency action should be subject to judicial review. Chapter 19 will examine this difficult but important area.

E. Section 705

Section 705 is straightforward. It reads as follows:

"When an agency finds that justice so requires, it may postpone the effective date of action taken by it, pending judicial review. On such conditions as may be required and to the extent necessary to prevent irreparable injury, the reviewing court, including the court to which a case may be taken on appeal from or on application for certiorari or other writ to a reviewing court, may issue all necessary and appropriate process to postpone the effective date of an agency action or to preserve status or rights pending conclusion of the review proceedings."

This section simply makes clear that both the agency and the reviewing court have the power to stay an agency action pending judicial review. This should strike you as familiar, given the well-known power of federal courts to issue stays, preliminary injunctions, and other types of temporary relief.

Before we conclude this chapter, let's take a look at how these sections of Chapter 7 build on each other. Section 701 begins by specifying when the rest of Chapter 7 applies. Section 702 sets forth who can be a party to the lawsuit (*i.e.*, who has standing to be a plaintiff and when the federal government can be the defendant). Section 703 speaks to what form that lawsuit takes. Section 704 speaks to when that lawsuit can be filed and heard. Section 705 makes clear that preliminary relief from an agency action is available. These preliminaries set us up for Section 706, which, as we'll see in Part Five, provides the rules governing what courts can do when they're ready to hear the merits of the case. But before we get to that question, the rest of Part Four will consider in more detail each of the issues presented in these earlier sections.

The short version: Chapter 7 of the APA creates a coherent structure that sets forth whether (Section 701), at whose behest (Section 702), in what forms (Section 703), and when (Section 704) an individual can challenge agency action. It also allows preliminary relief from an agency action subject to judicial review (Section 705).

CHAPTER 16

Reviewability

Section 701 of the APA considers when agency action will be subject to judicial review. As Chapter 15 stated, Section 701 defines "agency" broadly, as "each authority of the government of the United States," § 701(b)(1), but then excludes from that definition a number of such authorities, including Congress, the courts, the District of Columbia and U.S. possessions, and military courts, § 701(b)(1)(A)-(H). Thus, it includes the institutions we normally think about when we think about agencies, such as the EPA, the SEC, or the Department of the Interior.

For our purposes, the most important part of Section 701 speaks to when such "agency" action is subject to judicial review. Recall from Chapter 15 what Section 701 says about this:

"(a) This chapter applies, according to the provisions thereof, except to the extent that—

(1) statutes preclude judicial review; or

(2) agency action is committed to agency discretion by law."

By "[t]his chapter," Section 701 means Chapter 7 of the APA—the chapter that speaks to judicial review of agency action. Thus, the other provisions in Chapter 7 (Sections 702-706) apply in all cases challenging agency action, *except* when one of the two exceptions noted above exist. The Court has read these exceptions narrowly. As a result, we have come to use the phrase "the presumption of reviewability" to reflect the reality that, literally, it is presumed that judicial review will be available, unless one of these narrow exceptions is satisfied.

Let's now consider these two exceptions.

A. Statutory Preclusion

Begin with the exception for the situation in which "statutes preclude judicial review." As you can guess, this exception applies to situations in which the organic statute provides that a given agency action shall not be subject to judicial review. The Supreme Court has established that, in most cases, Congress must be exceptionally clear before such a "statute" will be held to "preclude judicial review." Thus, a statute that could be read as either precluding or not precluding review will more likely be read as not precluding review. Even statutes that seem clearly to preclude review will sometimes be read in more limited ways.

Consider, for example, *DeMore v. Kim*, 538 U.S. 510 (2003). *Kim* dealt with an immigration detainee's petition for a writ of habeas corpus, which claimed that an immigration agency's decision that the plaintiff's detention was mandatory under the relevant immigration laws violated his due process rights. The relevant statute, though, seemed fairly clearly to preclude judicial review:

"(e) Judicial Review

The Attorney General's discretionary judgment regarding the application of this section shall not be subject to review. No court may set aside any action or decision of the Attorney General under this section regarding the detention of any alien or the grant, revocation, or denial of bond or parole."

Sounds pretty conclusive, right? Nevertheless, a six-justice majority held that this subsection did *not* preclude the plaintiff's habeas corpus petition alleging a due process violation. Rather, it concluded that the statute did not speak to, and thus did not intend to preclude judicial review of, claims that the entire statutory framework was unconstitutional. Instead, it read the statute as simply precluding review of individualized decisions the Attorney General (or the immigration officials under his control) might make when administering the statute.

On the one hand, this analysis suggests simply that courts will often read seemingly preclusive language carefully to make sure that Congress indeed intended to preclude review of the type of claim the plaintiff was trying to bring. And that is an appropriate lesson from *Kim*. However, it might also be relevant that the claim in *Kim* was a constitutional claim, brought in the form of a habeas corpus petition. Such actions implicate the core role of Article III courts to ensure individual liberty (especially via habeas claims) and to vindicate constitutional rights (recall that the substance of the claim was that the statutory detention scheme violated the plaintiff's rights under the Due Process Clause). This latter reading of *Kim* suggests that courts will read statutory language as precluding judicial review more readily in some contexts than others. Indeed, consistent with *Kim*, it's been suggested that courts are more willing to find statutory preclusion when the claim is that the agency has simply misapplied the law to the plaintiff's particular case, and less willing to find preclusion when the claim implicates broader legal or even constitutional issues, or implicates a core function of Article III courts (for example, to review petitions for writs of habeas corpus).

Given this analysis, you might expect to be able to draw some other lessons about statutory preclusion. First, you might conclude that even if the organic statute provides for judicial review of some claims at the behest of some would-be plaintiffs, that does not necessarily mean that *other* claims brought by *other* would-be plaintiffs are therefore understood to be precluded by statute. Indeed, the Court has said as much. *See, e.g., Bowen v. Michigan Academy of Family Physicians*, 476 U.S. 667 (1986).

You might also be tempted to conclude that, given how difficult it is for a statute to preclude judicial review even when it's as explicit as the one in *Kim*, it would be almost impossible for a statute to be held to *implicitly* preclude judicial review. But not so fast: sometimes the Court has found exactly that sort of implied preclusion. As an example, consider *Block v. Community Nutrition Institute*, 467 U.S. 340 (1984). *Block* involved a challenge to the price set by the Department of Agriculture for dairy products, as part of an agricultural product price support scheme. Under that scheme, the Department would confer with representatives of particular groups identified in the relevant statute (for example, dairy farmers and wholesalers) to set the price for raw milk in a particular growing area of the country. If a member of one of those groups was dissatisfied with the agency's pricing decision, it would have to go through an extensive internal appeals process within the agency before it could sue in federal court.

Block featured a lawsuit by milk consumers, a group that was excluded from the price-setting process but that also was not mentioned in the mandatory internal appeals process. The Court held that the statute implicitly precluded lawsuits brought by consumers. Writing for the Court, Justice O'Connor explained that the system wouldn't make sense if a disfavored group—consumers—

who were not allowed into the price-setting process to begin with were allowed to bypass the internal agency appeals process and immediately seek Article III court review of the agency's decision. She acknowledged "the presumption of reviewability," but noted that that presumption "is just that—a presumption . . . [that] like all presumptions used in statutes, may be overcome by specific language or . . . inferences of [congressional] intent drawn from the statutory scheme as a whole."

Thus, it's certainly correct to conclude that there's a presumption of reviewability, and thus that statutes have to be clear before they're thought to preclude such review. It's also true that a statute's preclusive effect will be read narrowly. Nevertheless, context matters when considering whether and to what degree a statute will preclude judicial review. That context includes the type of claim made by the plaintiff, and the impact hearing that claim would have on the overall statutory scheme.

B. Preclusion Because Agency Action Is Committed to Agency Discretion by Law

Section 701's second exception—for agency action committed to agency discretion by law—is even more nuanced than statutory preclusion. On its face it's conceptually straightforward: if a law gives an agency discretion to act, then review is precluded. But ambiguities immediately appear. First, statutes give agencies discretion all the time—indeed, the very reason we have agencies is that there's a need for some institution to exercise discretion when making decisions implementing a complex statute. This exception cannot mean that there's no judicial review every time an agency exercises such discretion—if that were the case, the presumption of reviewability would be reversed into a presumption of unreviewability. Second, as we'll see in Part Five, a big part of courts' task when reviewing agency action is to determine whether an agency abused its discretion. How can a court strike down an agency action for abuse of "discretion" if all acts of "discretion" are unreviewable? Third, what does this exception mean when it says, "agency action committed to agency discretion *by law*"? How is "law" different from "statutes" in the first exception?

The foundational case for understanding this exception is *Citizens to Preserve Overton Park v. Volpe*, 401 U.S. 402 (1971). In *Overton Park* the Court stated that this exception is a narrow one, and applies to situations in which "statutes are drawn in such broad terms that in a given case there is no law to apply." In *Overton Park* itself the Court applied this idea to reject the argument made by the Department of Transportation that its decision to run a highway through a city park was unreviewable because that decision was "committed to agency discretion by law." The Court observed that the statute in question sought to prevent casual, unthinking use of parkland for highways, by allowing such use only if there was no "feasible and prudent" alternative. According to the Court, the statute's preference for not using parkland, and its insistence that such use be essentially the last reasonable option, meant that there was "law to apply," such that the agency's routing decision was subject to judicial review.

The "no law to apply" standard has remained the law. Nevertheless, it is important to note that the Court has applied that standard in somewhat broader ways than might be apparent from *Overton Park*. For example, consider *Heckler v. Chaney*, 470 U.S. 821 (1985). *Chaney* involved a request from a death row inmate that the Food and Drug Administration (FDA) investigate whether the state that was planning on executing him was planning on doing so by using drugs in ways unapproved by the FDA and thus in violation of federal law. When the agency declined his request the inmate sued.

The Court concluded that agency decisions declining to begin investigations or enforcement actions were presumptively unreviewable, as committed to the agency's discretion. In so concluding, the Court purported to apply the "no law to apply" standard. However, its analysis went a good deal beyond the obvious understanding of that term. For example, it noted the inherently discretionary nature of an agency's decisions to prioritize some potential regulatory violations over others when it came to allocating enforcement resources. It also noted how those decisions were analogous to law enforcement decisions more generally, decisions that, at the national level, were committed to the President and his Article II apparatus. The Court also observed that decisions not to enforce did not involve the agency bringing its coercive power to bear against a citizen, and thus carried less demand for judicial review.

The Court cautioned, however, that it was only concluding that such non-enforcement decisions were *presumptively* unreviewable, and noted that Congress could always overcome that presumption, say, by *requiring* that agencies investigate certain categories of possible illegal action. For our purposes, though, the larger point is that the "no law to apply" standard can be understood as including broader concerns about the general unsuitability of judicial review of certain types of agency action.

Indeed, in a post-*Chaney* case, *Webster v. Doe*, 486 U.S. 592 (1988), Justice Scalia, writing only for himself, argued that cases like *Chaney* illustrated that the "no law to apply" test was part of the correct approach to the "agency action committed to agency discretion by law" provision in Section 701, but was not the full understanding of that provision. He argued that that provision of Section 701 incorporated pre-APA judge-made administrative law, which inquired, just like *Chaney* did, into the general suitability of judicial review of particular agency decisions. According to Justice

Scalia, this pre-APA "administrative common law" was what the APA drafters meant when they spoke of "law," rather than "statutes," in Section 701(a)(2). It also explained how courts could review some agency actions for "abuse of discretion" while also acknowledging that some agency decisions were unreviewable exactly because they were "committed to agency discretion." Again, though, while Justice Scalia's more wide-ranging approach to "agency action committed to agency discretion by law" may be the one that is actually employed by courts, it's important to realize that the formal black-letter rule for this part of Section of 701 remains *Overton Park*'s "no law to apply" standard.

C. "Agency Action"

Before we leave this exception to Section 701, there's one more important point to be made. Recall that this exception refers to "agency action committed to agency discretion by law." So far, we've been focused on the latter part of this phrase, ignoring the "agency action" phrase with which it starts. But don't think that "agency action" is an obvious concept. It may seem like it is, but, like much in administrative law, it's a little more complicated than that. This is an important issue in administrative law; when you read Chapter 7 of the APA you'll encounter several references to that term. Understanding it is thus important to understanding when judicial review is available, and when it's not.

Start with the APA's definition of that term. Section 551 of the APA helpfully defines a variety of terms used throughout the statute. Definition 13 states that "agency action" "includes the whole or a part of an agency rule, order, license, sanction, relief, or the equivalent or denial thereof, or failure to act." This seems pretty comprehensive. But in *Norton v. Southern Utah Wilderness Alliance*, 542 U.S. 55 (2004), the Court gave it a more limited reading. *Southern Utah* involved claims made by environmentalists that the federal Bureau of Land Management (BLM) was mismanaging federal wilderness lands by allowing excessive use of off-road vehicles and other activities that degraded their wilderness qualities. The claim was thus that the agency was *failing* to act, by failing to manage the lands properly.

Of course, Definition 13 states that "agency action" includes "failure to act." Nevertheless, the Court concluded that "failure to act" means failure to take a discrete action—for example, failure to grant a license or promulgate a regulation—rather than failure to engage in ongoing oversight activities, such as proper land management. The Court reasoned that all of the Definition's examples of "action"—"rule, order, license, sanction, [and] relief"—were discrete. The Definition then included "the equivalent," which the Court read as equivalently discrete, "or the denial thereof," which again pointed back to the list of discrete actions. Thus, it concluded that a "failure to act" must be a failure to take a similarly discrete action.

The analysis may be intricate, but the rule is (somewhat) straightforward: agency action (or failure to act) consists only of an agency taking (or failing to take) a discrete action, rather than an agency's overall management (or failure to manage) a regulatory program. To repeat, this conclusion matters because, as we'll see in later chapters, "agency action" is used several times in Chapter 7 of the APA.

The short version: APA Section 701 has come to be understood as enacting a presumption that judicial review of agency action will be available, unless the organic statute precludes judicial review or the "agency action is committed to agency discretion by law." With regard to the first of these exceptions, courts will often strain to avoid reading a statute as precluding review, especially of legal or constitutional questions. The second of these exceptions has been interpreted as speaking to situations where statutes are written so broadly that "there is no law to apply." However, sometimes courts' applications of the "no law to apply" standard go beyond what one might assume from those words, to include more general inquiries into the suitability of that particular question for judicial review.

CHAPTER 17

Proper Parties to a Lawsuit: Standing and Sovereign Immunity

You may have studied standing in Constitutional Law or elsewhere in law school before coming into Administrative Law. Nevertheless, this chapter will discuss both the constitutional law aspects of standing and particular standing requirements that apply to challenges to agency action. Indeed, even the Article III standing requirements you might have studied earlier raise special problems when applied in administrative law. This chapter concludes with a quick look at sovereign immunity issues as they relate to administrative law.

A. Article III Standing

If you already studied standing, you'll recall that it seeks to determine whether the plaintiff has made out a "case or controversy" that is the business of an Article III court to hear. This requires that the plaintiff (1) be injured in a way that is both (2) caused by the defendant and (3) redressable by a court. That injury must be actual or imminent, particularized rather than generalized, and concrete rather than hypothetical or speculative. All three of these requirements are highly indefinite, and their application often generates significant controversy.

1. Injury

The Court has made clear that "injury" can take many forms. It can be an impairment of a traditional interest such as your bodily integrity (*e.g.*, if you're assaulted or falsely imprisoned) or chattel (*e.g.*, if your property has been destroyed or damaged). But it can mean more. For example, impairment of an aesthetic, recreational, or professional interest can also constitute injury. Thus, if a government action destroys your favorite hiking trail, that injury to your recreational interest can suffice to constitute injury. In addition, Congress can create rights, the deprivation of which constitutes Article III standing. For example, in *Havens Realty v. Coleman*, 455 U.S. 363 (1982), Black and white "testers" sought to determine whether rental agencies were complying with the federal Fair Housing Act (FHA) by acting like would-be renters with identical qualifications and housing needs, to determine whether the white tester was shown more housing options than the Black tester. Upon being told (allegedly falsely) that particular housing options were unavailable, the Black tester sued, claiming an impairment of the interest in truthful housing information, which the FHA gave him. The Court accepted that injury as adequate for Article III purposes.

Despite this seeming receptiveness, the injury requirement often trips up would-be plaintiffs. Consider, for example, *Lujan v. Defenders of Wildlife*, 504 U.S. 555 (1992). In *Defenders of Wildlife*, two wildlife researchers alleged that they were injured by the government's decision to assist foreign development projects that would threaten the species the researchers studied. While recognizing that impairment of their professional interests would constitute injury, the Court refused to find that injury sufficiently concrete or imminent, largely because the researchers admitted that they had no current definite plans to return to those countries to observe the species. A concurring opinion by Justice Kennedy conceded that it might seem odd or unduly formalistic to deny the plaintiffs standing on the ground that they had not yet purchased airplane tickets to return to the affected areas. Nevertheless, he insisted that lines had to be drawn in order to ensure that courts were not embroiled in deciding purely abstract disputes.

In later cases, the Court has had difficulty explaining how imminent an injury had to be for it to be "imminent" for Article III injury purposes. For example, in *Clapper v. Amnesty International USA*, 568 U.S. 398 (2013), the Court rejected the alleged injury on the ground that it neither currently existed nor was "certainly impending." In a footnote, however, it acknowledged that in other cases the Court did not require such certainty before a future injury would count for Article III purposes. Instead, in other cases it had merely required that there be a "substantial risk" that the harm will occur. This acknowledgement makes sense for administrative law, since many agency actions—for example, to promulgate a health regulation that is too lenient—may not be said to cause an injury that is "certainly impending." Rather, such regulations are often designed to do exactly what the Court's alternative allows for standing—to mitigate a "substantial risk" of harm.

Even more recent cases have considered the requirement that the plaintiff's injury be "concrete." Most notably, in *TransUnion v. Ramirez*, 141 S.Ct. 2190 (2021), the Court limited the category of injuries that would satisfy this requirement. In *TransUnion*, the Court held that a plaintiff did not have a concrete injury merely because a federal statute had given him a cause of action, or right to sue. *TransUnion* involved a credit reporting agency that had made mistakes on an individual's credit report. While the Court allowed plaintiffs in that situation to sue when the mistaken information had been disseminated to third parties (such as retailers running credit checks), it did not allow them to sue merely if the credit agency had created mistaken information, even though federal law allowed lawsuits in situations like that. The Court concluded that this latter injury (merely having mistaken credit information about oneself compiled) was not sufficiently concrete to count for Article III purposes. While congressional direction, in the form of statutes giving plaintiffs causes of action, provided guidance on the concreteness issue, the Court announced that it itself would be the final arbiter of what constitutes a sufficiently concrete injury.

A final issue with regard to injury deals with the requirement that the plaintiff's injury be particularized. In *Defenders of Wildlife*, the plaintiff-researchers claimed, as their final standing argument, that they were injured because they were being deprived of an interest Congress granted them. The source of that interest was the so-called "citizen suit" provision of the organic statute in question (the Endangered Species Act). That provision, as the title implies, gives any person the right to sue to challenge violations of the law. As we'll see when we talk about "statutory standing" in the next section of this chapter, such a provision clearly provides "any person" with a cause of action, and thus satisfies the requirement, discussed later, that a plaintiff have statutory standing. But the *Defenders of Wildlife* plaintiffs also argued that that same provision gave them *Article III* standing, because it reflected a congressional decision to give "every person" an interest in having the government comply with the law.

The Court rejected this latter use of the statute's citizen-suit provision. It acknowledged that Congress can create rights, the deprivation of which constitutes Article III injury. (For an example of this, see the discussion of the *Havens Realty* case, earlier in this section.) But the Court majority argued that the right the citizen-suit provision allegedly bestowed was one shared in equal measure by every American. Thus, when it was taken away by the allegedly-illegal agency action, that deprivation did not affect the plaintiffs in a particularized way.

Note that this analysis would not impact a plaintiff's standing in, say, a mass tort case such as an airplane crash. Many people may be injured by the defendant airline's conduct, but each injury (a death, a maiming, an experience of pain) would be unique and particularized to each plaintiff. By contrast, the Court argued in *Defenders of Wildlife*, the injury caused by deprivation of the right granted by the citizen-suit provision would be shared in equal measure by all Americans—essentially, it would be the same injury. For that reason, it did not constitute the type of individual injury that Article III courts were designed to redress.

In the years after *Defenders of Wildlife* the Court has struggled with the requirement of a particularized injury. In *Federal Election Commission v. Akins*, 524 U.S. 11 (1998), the Court suggested that some generalized grievances constitute injury for Article III purposes. However, in a footnote, a unanimous Court in *Lexmark Int'l v. Static Control Components*, 572 U.S. 118 (2014), described the generalized grievance bar as constitutional in nature.

2. *Causation and Redressability*

Causation and redressability also cause problems for plaintiffs. As you may have learned in Torts, causation can be a very elastic concept. In a sense, almost anything might be said to "cause" almost anything else. The Court has often required relatively tight causal connections between the injury and the defendant. Such a requirement often causes plaintiffs problems when their injury flows not directly from the government-defendant, but instead from a third party that the government is allegedly mis-regulating in a way that allows that third party to impose the injury on the plaintiff.

On this point, consider *Simon v. Eastern Kentucky Welfare Rights Org.*, 426 U.S. 26 (1976). In *Eastern Kentucky* indigent plaintiffs sued the Internal Revenue Service (IRS), alleging that it had misread the tax laws and thus had made it too easy for hospitals to retain charity status while still refusing to provide free or low-cost care. (Charity status is desirable because it allows contributions to that institution to be tax deductible.) The Court denied standing. It concluded that it was not sufficiently clear that it was the IRS that caused the injury, since, even if it had imposed tougher requirements for charity status it was still possible that the hospitals would simply decide that that status wasn't worth the cost and would continue to deny the plaintiffs the care they desired.

Put another way, under this analysis it was not clear that a court could redress the plaintiffs' injury, since, again, an injunction against the IRS requiring it to toughen up its charity criteria would not help the plaintiffs if the hospitals responded to the tougher requirements by simply deciding to forego charity status. (If you're wondering why the plaintiffs didn't sue the hospitals instead, since they were the ones directly injuring them, think about it some more—the plaintiffs had no legal claim against the hospitals. The only entity that might have been violating the law in this example was the IRS, by mis-implementing federal tax laws.) Of course, it's just as possible that it really was the IRS that was "causing" the injury, and that an injunction against it would indeed have redressed the injury. The Court in *Eastern Kentucky* simply insisted on more proof of that claim.

Another redressability issue is whether civil penalties paid to the government can redress a plaintiff's injury. In *Friends of the Earth v. Laidlaw Environmental Services*, 528 U.S. 167 (2000), the Court considered an argument that such penalties did not redress the private plaintiff's injury, with the result that the plaintiff lacked standing when such penalties were the only remedy allowed. The

Court held that Congress could reasonably decide that such civil penalties would deter future conduct of the sort that the plaintiffs were complaining of (in this case, pollution of a stream), and thus would redress injuries that conduct imposed on the plaintiffs. The dissenters in that case argued that this sort of structure allowed private parties to in effect usurp the agency's law enforcing role, and thus disrupt the agency's Article II-based power to enforce violations of that statute.

Thus, the three constitutional requirements—injury, causation, and redressability—are malleable and difficult to establish (or prove the absence of) in any objective way. Standing questions will often be matters of judgment and degree, and may call for you to reason by analogy to the cases you've read.

3. *Associational Standing*

One important component of standing law for administrative law purposes speaks to when an association can sue on behalf of its members. (Of course, an association can always sue on its own behalf: if an organization is defrauded or otherwise injured it can always sue to recover its own losses. We're speaking instead of an association suing on behalf of its members.) This is an important branch of standing law for administrative law purposes, because, as you may have noticed, many administrative law plaintiffs are associations—either industry groups (*e.g.*, the Motor Vehicle Manufacturers' Association) or public interest groups, such as the Sierra Club or Defenders of Wildlife, which was the actual plaintiff in the *Defenders of Wildlife* case discussed earlier in this chapter.

The test for associational standing is straightforward and based in common sense (although, as you'll see, the first prong incorporates all the uncertainties and ambiguities we've discussed up to now). For an association to sue on behalf of its members, it must satisfy the following three requirements:

1. At least one member of the association must have been able to demonstrate standing on her own part;

2. The association exists for reasons that are germane to the lawsuit; and

3. The relief the association seeks must be effective in redressing the individual member's injury, despite that member's absence as a named plaintiff.

Think about these requirements. As for the first one, it makes sense that, since the association is suing on behalf of one (or more) of its members, at least one of those members must have been able to sue on her own had she wished. Essentially, somebody on the plaintiff's side has to satisfy the injury, causation, and redressability requirements discussed above. Of course, this means that all those requirements' ambiguities apply to associational standing. Again, recall that the researchers discussed earlier in *Defenders of Wildlife* had to show standing in order for the Defenders of Wildlife organization to sue on their behalf.

As for the second requirement, it again makes perfect sense to require that the association have some connection to the subject-matter of the lawsuit. Assume, for example, that one of the researchers in *Defenders of Wildlife* was getting a divorce or had been involved in a traffic accident. There's no reason to think that a wildlife protection association would be a particularly good plaintiff to bring that sort of claim on the researcher's behalf.

Finally, consider the final requirement. As a general matter, what this requirement means is that an association will generally be able to sue an agency for an injunction requiring the agency to do something or forbidding it from doing something. Because the injunction can operate to the benefit of the entire world, it would likely redress the injury suffered by the individual member. By contrast, if the association sought damages, the absence of the injured member as a formal party to the lawsuit might give the court second thoughts about whether a damages award would in fact redress that member's injury, because it might doubt its ability to ensure that the damages check actually made it to the plaintiff. Again, the implication of this latter rule is that injunctive relief is generally open to associations suing on behalf of their members, but damages awards are not. (To repeat, if the association was suing on *its own* behalf, of course it could seek damages—say, for being defrauded.)

B. Statutory/Zone of Interest Standing

In addition to Article III requirements, a plaintiff seeking to challenge agency action must demonstrate so-called "statutory" standing. Another way of thinking about this requirement is by recognizing that such a plaintiff needs to demonstrate that Congress gave him a cause of action to sue.

There are two sources of law for determining whether a plaintiff has such a cause of action. First, one can look to the organic statute to determine whether it provides a cause of action. The organic statute might authorize certain types of parties—for example, unsuccessful applicants for a license issued by the agency—to sue to challenge the agency's denial of their applications. More generally, a statute could feature a citizen-suit provision of the sort mentioned earlier in this chapter, in the discussion of *Defenders of Wildlife*. Such a statute, by giving every person a right to sue, provides a cause of action that satisfies the statutory standing requirement.

Sometimes, however, a plaintiff will not find either sort of explicit cause of action in the organic statute. That doesn't mean the plaintiff is out of luck. Rather, that plaintiff needs to look at Section 702 of the APA. Section 702 begins with the following sentence: "A person suffering legal wrong because of agency action, or adversely affected or aggrieved by agency action within the meaning of a relevant statute, is entitled to judicial review thereof." It thus speaks to who is "entitled to judicial review"—that is, who is allowed to sue.

Section 702 begins by allowing standing for a person "suffering legal wrong because of agency action." Thus, a person whose legal rights have been impaired by an agency action—for example, a person who has a legal right to a benefit but has been denied it—has a cause of action under Section 702. Section 702 also allows standing for a person "adversely affected or aggrieved by agency action within the meaning of a relevant statute." In *Association of Data Processing Service Organizations v. Camp*, 397 U.S. 150 (1970), the Court interpreted this latter phrase as requiring that the plaintiff be "arguably within the zone of interests to be protected or regulated by the [relevant] statute." In *Data Processors* and later cases, the Court has made clear that the "zone of interests" test is not difficult to satisfy. For example, in *Data Processors* itself, the Court held that a group representing data processing companies had zone of interests standing to challenge an agency regulation that made it easier for banks to provide data processing services for bank clients. The regulation increased the competition the data processing companies faced, but the banking statute on which the agency regulation rested did not explicitly reflect an intention to benefit those data processors. Nevertheless, the fact that the banking statute aimed to limit banks to the general business of banking necessarily meant that data processor competitors of banks were "arguably within the zone of interests" the banking statute sought to protect.

In fact, the Supreme Court has held the zone of interests test to be unsatisfied in only one case, *Air Courier Conference of America v. American Postal Workers Union*, 498 U.S. 517 (1991). *Air Courier* involved a challenge brought by a union of postal workers against a regulation allowing private mail delivery companies to deposit mail with foreign postal services. The Court held that the postal workers lacked zone of interests standing in part because the original postal statutes were enacted at a time when there were no postal workers. Thus, the Court reasoned, it was impossible to conclude that postal workers were even arguably with the zone of interests that statute protected.

If *Air Courier* is hard to understand as an application of what the Court describes as an easy-to-satisfy test, perhaps more light is shone on the issue by another case, *Lujan v. National Wildlife Federation*, 497 U.S. 871 (1990). (Note that this is a different case from *Lujan v. Defenders of Wildlife*, discussed earlier in this chapter.) In *National Wildlife*, the Court posed the hypothetical of a law that required an agency to engage in formal adjudication. The Court explained that if the agency ignored that legal mandate, a firm that provided stenography services would not have zone of interest standing, even if it might be able to show Article III standing. The Court explained that, since the formal adjudication mandate was obviously imposed for the benefit of the persons who would be parties to those formal adjudications, rather than the benefit of the company that created the stenographic record of those proceedings, such a company would not even arguably fall within the zone of interests the statute sought to protect.

C. Sovereign Immunity

In contrast to standing, federal sovereign immunity poses relatively simple issues for most students of administrative law. The text of Section 702 makes clear that sovereign immunity does not stand in the way of plaintiffs seeking to sue an agency for injunctive relief, such as an order enjoining an agency from enforcing a regulation (or, if the agency has failed to act, say, by failing to promulgate a regulation within a statutorily-mandated period, an order compelling the agency to promulgate that regulation). "Money damages," however, are not available under Section 702's waiver of sovereign immunity. (Again, if Congress chooses, it may waive that immunity in the organic statute.) But note one thing: the bar on "money damages" doesn't mean that all claims that involve money are barred by sovereign immunity. For example, if a statute requires that a particular amount be paid to someone (say, a medical provider under the federal Medicare program), then a plaintiff could seek a court order requiring the agency to pay the correct amount. As long as the order to pay is not compensatory in nature—that is, as long as it's not a "damages" award—a court can issue it consistent with Section 702.

The short version: A plaintiff challenging an agency's action in federal court must satisfy Article III's standing requirements. This can be difficult if the plaintiff's injury flows not from the agency directly, but instead from the agency's alleged mis-regulation of a third party which thereby allows that third party to injure the plaintiff. In addition, a plaintiff must have statutory standing, or, as is sometimes said, she must have a statutory cause of action. If the organic statute does not provide that statutory right to sue, the plaintiff can often find it in APA Section 702, which has been interpreted to give persons the right to sue an agency if they are "arguably within the zone of interests sought to be protected" by the organic statute. Associations seeking to sue agencies on behalf of their members face a specialized standing test, which requires (1) that one member have standing, (2) that the subject-matter of the lawsuit be germane to the association, and (3) that the relief sought would be effective in the absence of the injured member. Sovereign immunity poses few hurdles for plaintiffs, as Section 702 waives federal sovereign immunity except for claims seeking "money damages."

CHAPTER 18

The Form of Proceeding and Jurisdiction

Section 703 is generally straightforward. For our purposes, it reflects two important concepts. First, it provides that the form of action one uses to challenge an agency action is either (1) the review proceeding authorized by the organic statute or (2) in the absence or inadequacy of that proceeding, "any applicable form of legal action," "including actions for declaratory judgments or writs of prohibitory or mandatory injunction or habeas corpus." The first of these possibilities reflects the fact that modern organic statutes often prescribe the type of action that one can bring in order to challenge the agency's action. However, if the organic statute does not include such a provision, or if that provision is inadequate, then the plaintiff may use whatever legal proceeding would provide the desired relief, for example, an action for a declaratory judgment. The general idea here is that the APA attempts to make possible whatever legal action would make the plaintiff whole, while also respecting Congress's choice to provide particular routes to judicial review.

Second, however, note that Section 703 allows "any applicable form of legal action . . . *in a court of competent jurisdiction*." (emphasis added). The italicized language makes clear that Section 703 by itself does not confer statutory jurisdiction on a federal court to hear a challenge to an agency action. Instead, the plaintiff must look to the organic statute, which might provide that jurisdiction, or, failing that, some other more general grant of statutory jurisdiction, such as that in 28 U.S.C. § 1331 (the general federal question jurisdiction statute).

Of course, a party who wishes to challenge an agency action, for example a regulation, could simply sit back and wait for the agency to try to enforce that action against the party, and then defend on the ground that the action is illegal. The last sentence of Section 703 makes clear that such relief is usually available. (Take a look at Section 703, either in your book or Chapter 15 of this *Guide*, to see that language.) Of course, this strategy is risky: defiance of an agency action that is ultimately upheld means that the party would be liable for whatever sanctions that could be imposed for that violation. This dilemma is further explored in the discussion of the *Abbott Labs* case in the next chapter's examination of ripeness doctrine.

The short version: APA Section 703 provides that the organic statute's form of proceeding should be the one a plaintiff uses to challenge that agency's action, unless that form is inadequate or doesn't exist. In that case, Section 703 allows the plaintiff to use any form of proceeding that would provide the plaintiff with effective relief. However, neither Section 703 nor the APA more generally provides courts with statutory jurisdiction. For such jurisdiction, courts must look either to the agency's organic statute or, failing that, to a more general statutory jurisdictional grant, such as the general federal question jurisdiction statute.

CHAPTER 19

Timing Issues and Preliminary Relief

There are three important doctrines that speak to the timing of a challenge to an agency action. First, such a challenge must be ripe. Second, the APA allows parties to challenge "final agency action." Third, a person must normally exhaust her administrative remedies before bringing suit in court.

These doctrines are very closely related. Indeed, an appellate decision once held that the plaintiff's lawsuit was premature, but the three judges on the panel each identified a different one of the three timing doctrines identified above in support for that decision. *Ticor Title, Inc. v. FTC*, 814 F.2d 731 (D.C. Cir. 1987). Thus, you should not try too hard to separate them out. Nevertheless, conceptually, one can perhaps say that ripeness doctrine is court-centered, in that it looks to whether the matter is one that is appropriately decided by a court at that point in time, while "finality" looks to the agency, and whether it has reached a final decision that is ready for judicial challenge, and while exhaustion looks to the plaintiff, and considers whether she should be forced to exhaust her administrative remedies. Again though, and as you'll see in this chapter, these doctrines are closely related. This chapter concludes with brief discussions of a doctrine called "primary jurisdiction" and of Section 705, which deals with preliminary relief from an agency action.

A. Ripeness

Ripeness doctrine asks whether a case is "ripe" for judicial decision, or, conversely, whether it is too early for the court to hear the case. You may have studied ripeness in Constitutional Law, because, as we'll see, this doctrine is partly based on Article III concerns about whether a challenge has "ripened" to the point where it constitutes a "case or controversy" of the type appropriate for judicial resolution. But ripeness also rests on more prudential concerns. The distinction between these groundings for a ripeness decision has implications for Congress's ability to require early, "pre-enforcement" review of agency action.

The modern law of ripeness dates from *Abbott Labs v. Gardner*, 387 U.S. 136 (1967). In *Abbott Labs*, the Court explained that ripeness is comprised of two inquiries: (1) whether the case is fit for judicial resolution at that point in time, and (2) what the hardship to the parties would be if the court deferred review to a future time. It suggested that the first prong spoke to whether the case had "ripened" into a case or controversy that was appropriate for an Article III court to decide, thus indicating that this prong is of constitutional dimension. As will be explained below, the hardship prong, by contrast, speaks more to prudential concerns about when it is a good idea for a court to decide a case immediately, and when, by contrast, it is appropriate for the court to wait.

Abbott Labs dealt with a regulation promulgated by the Food and Drug Administration (FDA) requiring that drug manufacturers include several pieces of information on product labels. Before the regulation was enforced against any particular manufacturer, a manufacturer sued, arguing that the agency's organic statute did not authorize that regulation.

The Court held that the challenge was ripe. Addressing the "fitness" question, the Court noted that the regulation constituted final agency action. (Note how the Court's conclusion about finality influenced its ripeness analysis.) It also explained that the challenge presented a purely legal question—whether the statute authorized the agency's regulation. Thus, there was nothing about the case that would have made a decision easier or more accurate had there existed the surrounding factual context of an enforcement action.

Turning to the "hardship" prong, the Court noted that the regulation put drug manufacturers in a difficult position: a manufacturer could either comply and incur the cost of destroying existing labels that lacked the newly-required information, or it could defy the agency and run the risk of the agency accusing the manufacturer of selling adulterated or unsafe drugs. Given the public concern about safe drugs, the Court concluded that this choice constituted a significant hardship for the plaintiff.

The Court sharpened the effect of its holding in *Abbott Labs* by deciding another ripeness case that very same day, *Toilet Goods Association v. Gardner*, 387 U.S. 158 (1967), where the Court held that the challenge was not ripe. *Toilet Goods* dealt with a regulation, also promulgated by the FDA. The *Toilet Goods* regulation authorized the agency to suspend any manufacturer's "certification services" for color additives it used for its products if that manufacturer failed to admit a government official who wished to inspect the firm's production facilities. Such a "certification" was required for the manufacturer to sell its products.

Applying the same two-pronged analysis as in *Abbott Labs*, the Court first conceded that, in some way, the regulation in *Toilet Goods*, just like the one in *Abbott Labs*, presented a purely legal question—whether the organic statute authorized the regulation in question. However, the Court explained that in *Toilet Goods* that legal question—whether the regulation was appropriate "for the efficient enforcement" of the organic statute—required an understanding of the problems the agency was encountering in enforcing the statute, and how the inspection/certification suspension regulation aided the agency in that enforcement. Because the *Toilet Goods* case was brought before there was such a demand for an inspection, and thus before a manufacturer's refusal and in turn before the agency's invocation of the certification suspension authority, the Court did not have the information it needed in order to answer that underlying legal question, and would likely not obtain it until such a chain of events actually occurred.

With regard to the hardship prong, the Court explained that, unlike in *Abbott Labs*, there would be no serious hardship to the party if it was required to wait to bring its challenge until it was the subject of an enforcement action. Unlike the regulation in *Abbott Labs*, the *Toilet Goods* regulation, by itself, did not force any party to do or refrain from doing anything. Indeed, it was possible that, if the agency never sought to inspect a manufacturer's facility, it would never feel the effect of the regulation's grant of authority to the agency to suspend certification services.

Taken together, *Abbott Labs* and *Toilet Goods* reveal not just the two-part legal test for ripeness, but how that test plays out, with different results, in two similar but distinct fact patterns. The Court's analysis in *Abbott Labs* also has implications for what Congress can do—and what it can't do—with regard to influencing the timing of judicial review. Today, Congress will often allow or even require that any challenges to an agency regulation be brought within a set period of time (for example, 60 days) after the regulation was promulgated. Such statutory "pre-enforcement review" (the term comes from the idea of having a court review the regulation "pre-enforcement," that is, before the agency enforces the regulation) will sometimes encounter the objection that, whatever Congress may allow or even command, the challenge in question simply isn't ripe. To the extent that ripeness decision is based on non-constitutional, prudential considerations, Congress's contrary determination is usually thought to govern. Thus, in that case the court's ripeness concerns would be overridden by Congress's pre-enforcement review mandate. By contrast, if the court's ripeness concerns rest on Article III-based questions, then a contrary congressional command does not govern. But what happens if the time period (say, the 60 days in our example) runs out before the court is ready to consider the case ripe? In that case, courts will usually toll that time period (*i.e.*, the clock will be held not to start to run) until a court is in fact ready to consider the case ripe.

B. Finality

Finality is another timing doctrine, one based in Section 704. Recall how Section 704 starts: "Agency action made reviewable by statute and final agency action for which there is no other adequate remedy in a court are subject to judicial review." The first part of this sentence makes clear that the organic statute can always make a particular type of agency action subject to judicial review (assuming the case is ripe, as discussed in the previous section). But even in the absence of the organic statute explicitly making a type of agency action reviewable, "final agency action for which there is no other adequate remedy in a court" is also "subject to judicial review." This raises the question, what constitutes "final agency action"?

The modern rule for "finality" comes from *Bennett v. Spear*, 520 U.S. 154 (1997). In *Bennett* the Court held that finality requires two things: (1) the action in question must mark the culmination of the agency's decisional process, and (2) legal consequences must flow from that action.

The first of these requirements is conceptually very straightforward: essentially, it demands that the action in question be the final considered view of the agency, rather than one that is still under consideration. This makes perfect sense: it makes no sense to call an action "final" and thus to allow judicial review of it if the agency might ultimately select a different action. Of course, no action is ever really final: as a lower court thinking about the finality requirement once observed, even the U.S. Constitution is subject to amendment. Nevertheless, in many cases it should be clear whether the action represents the agency's conclusive settling on a particular view or answer to a question even if, of course, that answer is always subject to revision tomorrow.

The second of these prongs is more troublesome. Of course, we can understand how some regulatory actions have legal consequences. Think of the regulation in *Abbott Labs*: from the second that regulation was promulgated, companies were legally required to change their labelling, and if they didn't they were in violation of federal law. On the other hand, a smart lawyer will understand that even an agency statement that doesn't purport to be formally legally binding might still prompt a cautious regulated party to change its conduct. After all, even if the agency says, for example, that a particular interpretation of a statute represents nothing more than the agency's litigating position, or its presumptive, but not conclusive approach to every situation where it might apply, the message the agency sends is still a powerful one, and a lawyer would be foolish to tell her client not to worry since the agency action isn't formally legally binding.

Courts understand this, and will sometimes read the legally-binding prong of *Bennett* in a very flexible way that takes account of this reality. For example, in a lower court case dealing with a guidance document issued by the Environmental Protection Agency, the court concluded that the document did in fact have legal consequences even though it explicitly stated that it did not. *Appalachian Power Company v. Environmental Protection Agency*, 208 F.3d 1015 (D.C. Cir. 2000). According to the court, the document's detailed nature and use of mandatory language strongly suggested to regulated parties that the agency was expecting compliance, and thus that the document did indeed have legal consequences. More recently, in *U.S. Army Corps of Engineers v. Hawkes*, 578 U.S. 590 (2016), the Supreme Court emphasized the "pragmatic" character of the finality requirement. In particular, it stated that that second requirement could be met when an agency action exposes a party to an increased risk of consequences that are not yet legally mandated.

C. Exhaustion

As explained at the start of this chapter, exhaustion refers to the requirement that a would-be plaintiff go through (or "exhaust") any remedies the agency provides to challenge an agency action before that plaintiff can sue in federal court. The exhaustion requirement is based on good common sense. As courts have explained, requiring exhaustion gives the agency the chance to correct any errors it might have made at a lower level or earlier stage, thus obviating the need for courts to step in. Even if federal court intervention is ultimately required, requiring exhaustion allows the agency to use its expertise to sharpen the issues the court needs to decide, and perhaps to provide a fuller factual record. Finally, requiring exhaustion respects both the agency and whatever regulatory scheme, including internal agency appeals, that Congress may have seen fit to establish.

Having said all this, note what exhaustion is *not* about. It is not about Article III-based limits on federal court action. Thus, exhaustion has been understood to be a purely judge-made prudential doctrine, to which either courts themselves or Congress can prescribe exceptions.

Consistent with exhaustion doctrine's nature as grounded in good judicial common-sense, exceptions to the exhaustion requirement reflect those same types of policy concerns. Thus, in non-APA cases, the Supreme Court has held that a failure to exhaust should be excused if the agency adjudication scheme raises a risk of unfair prejudice to the individual's claim (say, because of harsh timing requirements), if the agency is not authorized to provide the type of relief (for example, damages) that the individual seeks, or if the agency decision-maker is shown to be biased against the claimant. *See McCarthy v. Madigan*, 503 U.S. 140 (1992) (announcing and applying these factors).

Section 704 of the APA speaks to exhaustion in cases brought under the APA. It limits the exhaustion requirement to certain situations. It does this through the (convoluted) last sentence of Section 704:

> "Except as otherwise expressly required by statute, agency action otherwise final is final for the purposes of this section whether or not there has been presented or determined an application for a declaratory order, for any form of reconsideration, or, unless the agency otherwise requires by rule and provides that the action meanwhile is inoperative, for an appeal to superior agency authority."

For our purposes, we can remove certain language from this sentence to get to the gist of what Section 704 says about exhaustion. Removing the extraneous language and moving one of the phrases to an earlier position for readability results in the following provision:

> "Except as otherwise expressly required by statute, agency action otherwise final is final for the purposes of this section whether or not there has been presented or determined an application [for an appeal to superior agency authority], unless the agency otherwise requires by rule and provides that the action meanwhile is inoperative."

The thrust of this part of the provision is that exhaustion is not required (*i.e.*, "agency action otherwise final is final" and thus subject to judicial review) "whether or not there has been presented an application" "for an appeal to superior agency authority" "unless the agency otherwise requires [exhaustion] by rule and provides that the action meanwhile is inoperative." Boiling this language down even further yields the following rule: exhaustion is not required unless the agency (1) requires exhaustion (2) by rule and (3) provides that the preliminary result of that action is stayed. Think about what this means: an agency is authorized to require exhaustion, but only if it does so by promulgating a generally-applicable regulation requiring it, which also provides that the appealed-from result is inoperative during the pendency of that internal agency appeal. Thus, for example, an ALJ cannot require exhaustion solely on his own motion as part of his decision of the case, even if that ALJ stays his ruling pending that internal appeal.

In *Darby v. Cisneros*, 509 U.S. 137 (1993), the Court held that this rule from Section 704 constitutes the full rule for requiring exhaustion in APA cases, unless the organic statute includes its own rules about exhaustion. (This latter caveat is based on the first phrase of Section 704, "Except as otherwise expressly required by statute"—note again that the APA is only a default and that Congress can always prescribe different rules for a particular regulatory program by including those different rules in the organic statute.)

Thus, after *Darby*, a court hearing a case brought under the APA cannot supplement Section 704's exhaustion requirements with additional judge-made requirements.

D. Primary Jurisdiction

One relatively obscure judicial doctrine, called "primary jurisdiction," authorizes a court hearing a case not involving an agency to remit a particular issue to the relevant agency for it to make an initial decision. This doctrine becomes relevant when the decision of a case otherwise properly before a court would benefit from a preliminary decision by an agency. One can easily understand the relationship of this doctrine to exhaustion, given that they share the same underlying idea—namely, that it may make good sense for a court to stay its hand before acting if an agency has not yet had an opportunity to consider the issue.

E. Preliminary Relief

Finally, Section 705 addresses the availability of preliminary relief. This section requires little discussion, because it clearly authorizes both the agency as well as a reviewing court to stay an agency's action pending, respectively, judicial review or the court's final decision on the issue.

The short version: There are three main timing issues affecting cases challenging agency action. First, such a case must be ripe. Ripeness is a judge-made doctrine that asks whether (1) the question is fit for judicial resolution at that early stage and (2) there would be hardships to one or both parties if the court delayed its hearing of the case. The first of these requirements rests on Article III concerns about courts' power to hear only "cases and controversies;" by contrast, the second factor is more prudential rather than constitutionally-grounded. Second, APA Section 704 allows judicial review of any agency action the organic statute makes reviewable, and also "final agency action" for which there is no other adequate remedy. "Finality" requires (1) that the action be one that represents the agency's final position on that issue and (2) that legal consequences flow from that decision. Third, a plaintiff is often required to "exhaust" her administrative remedies before suing. APA Section 704 provides that exhaustion is required in an APA case only if the agency requires exhaustion by rule and only if that rule also provides that the appealed-from decision will be stayed during the pendency of that internal agency appeal.

* * * * *

THE TAKEAWAY

What are the main issues this Part addresses?

- The availability of judicial review of agency action under the APA.

  There is a presumption that agency action is subject to judicial review unless the organic statute precludes judicial review or "agency action is committed to agency discretion by law." These exceptions are read narrowly.

- The requirements for standing to sue an agency.

  Plaintiffs seeking to sue an agency must satisfy Article III's standing requirements. They must also have a cause of action, which could come either from the organic statute or if, pursuant to APA Section 702, they are "arguably within the zone of interests" sought to be protected by the organic statute.

- Where a federal court finds statutory jurisdiction to hear a challenge to agency action.

  The APA does not provide such jurisdiction. Rather, the court can assert jurisdiction either based on the organic statute (if it provides it) or, if it doesn't, in a more general jurisdictional statute such as 28 U.S.C. § 1331.

- **The timing requirements for a lawsuit challenging agency action.**

A lawsuit challenging agency action must be ripe. Ripeness doctrine includes both constitutional and prudential aspects. In addition, either the organic statute must make the action reviewable or the action must be "final agency action" within the meaning of APA Section 704. Finally, a plaintiff is generally required to exhaust her administrative remedies before suing in federal court, although Section 704 prescribes what an agency must do it if wishes to insist on such exhaustion in a case brought under the APA.

Judicial Review of Agency Action

Part Five of this *Guide* discusses the standards courts use when reviewing the substance of agency action. Of course, courts also review the *process* by which agencies act, as we saw in the cases discussed in Parts Two and Three. But those cases do not involve difficult decisions about the standards governing that review. By contrast, when courts review the output of those processes—that is, the actual regulatory results—difficult questions arise regarding the proper standard of judicial review.

Part Five deals with those questions. After an introductory chapter (Chapter 20) discussing APA Section 706—the source of courts' authority to perform such judicial review—it then considers, in Chapter 21, judicial review of agency fact-findings. It then considers judicial review of agency legal interpretations, in Chapter 22. Finally, it considers judicial review of agency policy-making, in Chapter 23.

One caveat as you begin to read these chapters. We sometimes assume that fact-finding, law-interpreting, and policy-making are completely distinct functions, with no overlap. As we'll see, they're not. This will complicate our examination of how courts review agencies' performance of each function, since, as it turns out, those functions tend to bleed into each other. As you study this material, it will be important to keep these functions distinct in your mind while at the same time recognizing their interrelatedness.

Section 706 of the APA

Section 706 of the APA is the section that gives courts the authority to strike down (or compel) agency action. It bears beginning this Part's discussion of judicial review of the substance of agency action by looking at Section 706 in more detail before doing the function-by-function investigation explained in the Introduction to Part Five.

Section 706 reads as follows:

"To the extent necessary to decision and when presented, the reviewing court shall decide all relevant questions of law, interpret constitutional and statutory provisions, and determine the meaning or applicability of the terms of an agency action. The reviewing court shall—

(1) compel agency action unlawfully withheld or unreasonably delayed; and

(2) hold unlawful and set aside agency action, findings, and conclusions found to be—

   (A) arbitrary, capricious, an abuse of discretion, or otherwise not in accordance with law;

(B) contrary to constitutional right, power, privilege, or immunity;

(C) in excess of statutory jurisdiction, authority, or limitations, or short of statutory right;

(D) without observance of procedure required by law;

(E) unsupported by substantial evidence in a case subject to sections 556 and 557 of this title or otherwise reviewed on the record of an agency hearing provided by statute; or

(F) unwarranted by the facts to the extent that the facts are subject to trial de novo by the reviewing court.

In making the foregoing determinations, the court shall review the whole record or those parts of it cited by a party, and due account shall be taken of the rule of prejudicial error."

Note several things. First, the section begins by giving the reviewing court the power to "decide all relevant questions of law." When we get to judicial review of legal interpretations, in Chapter 22, we'll have to consider how we can square this authority with the deference courts often show to agency statutory interpretations.

Next, note that Section 706 gives courts the power both to "set aside" (that is, strike down) agency action and to compel agency action (if it's unlawfully withheld or unreasonably delayed), when the challenged action or inaction comes under one of the subsequent six categories. Sometimes you'll encounter situations where agencies fail to act in a way a court concludes is unlawful (for example, by failing to promulgate a regulation within the time frame mandated by Congress). Don't think that courts' sole authority is to strike down agency action. (But by the same token, don't forget the discussion of what constitutes "agency action" or "failure to act," in Chapter 16.)

These preliminaries bring us to the six categories of justifications for compelling or striking down agency action. As you'll see, the remaining chapters in Part Five will focus a lot on three of these justifications—subsections (A), (C), and (E). This chapter will explain why those subsections take up the lion's share of our discussion in the chapters that follow.

First, let's walk through the other subsections. Subsection (B) straightforwardly authorizes courts to review agency action for constitutionality. This shouldn't surprise you, given how critical review for constitutionality is, as a general matter, to the role of the Article III courts. Don't be surprised at the prospect that agencies might have so much authority that they might do something unconstitutional. Just to take three quick examples, an agency action can discriminate on usually-forbidden grounds (such as race), it can impair a fundamental right (for example, if an immigration agency detains a citizen at the border), and it can deny someone the process that is guaranteed by the Fifth Amendment's Due Process Clause. These simple examples should make clear that review for constitutionality is a real prospect in administrative law.

Subsection (D) should not surprise you either. By now you've seen many examples of courts striking down agency action for failure to follow the proper procedure, both statutory (for example, Section 553's rulemaking requirements) and constitutional (the procedures required by the Fifth Amendment's Due Process Clause).

By contrast, subsection (F) may not ring a bell with you. That subsection contemplates not just *de novo* review (*i.e.*, review with no deference) by an Article III court, but a completely new fact-finding process at the reviewing court. Thus, subsection (F) contemplates, essentially, the reviewing court starting all over again with regard to fact-finding, calling the witnesses again and doing all the other things implied by the concept of "trial *de novo*" (rather than simply *de novo* review). Thankfully, you will likely not encounter many situations in which this subsection applies. Subsection (F) hearkens back to pre-APA case law where it was sometimes thought that some questions were so critical to the agency's constitutional authority to act that the facts supporting that authority had to be re-found by the Article III court after a brand-new trial in that court. That case law has largely been abandoned except in extremely specialized areas, and unless your professor focuses on it, it's something you can probably safely de-emphasize.

Thus, subsections (B) and (D) are intuitive, but apply only to particular situations (respectively, claims of unconstitutional or procedurally bad agency action), while subsection (F) is largely irrelevant today. That leaves us with subsections (A), (C), and (E). Let's think about those three situations. Subsection (C) applies in an important, but nevertheless discrete, area of law—the area dealing with claims that the agency has misinterpreted its organic statute. We'll deal with this particular area in Chapter 22.

That leaves us with subsections (A) and (E). Subsection (E) deals with a particularized situation—one in which the agency action in question is "subject to sections 556 and 557 of this title or otherwise reviewed on the record of an agency hearing provided by statute." Note the language "on the record of an agency hearing." Recall also the APA sections this subsection refers back to—Sections 556 and 557. All of these references suggest a formal agency hearing. Thus, subsection (E), which authorizes courts to strike down action that's "unsupported by substantial evidence," applies when the agency has acted through a formal agency action. That action can be fact-finding, or policy-making. As long as fact-finding or policy-making emerged from a formal process, then it is reviewed under the "substantial evidence" standard.

This leaves us with everything else—that is, agency action that doesn't involve constitutional or statutory interpretation claims, claims of bad procedure, or formalized agency action. In that broad catch-all category, subsection (A) applies. Thus, the kind of review contemplated by subsection (A)—what has become shorthanded as "arbitrary and capricious" review—is the default standard, applicable when none of the other standards applies. We'll talk a lot about "arbitrary and capricious" review in Chapter 23.

There's one final piece to Section 706: "In making the foregoing determinations, the court shall review the whole record or those parts of it cited by a party, and due account shall be taken of the rule of prejudicial error." We'll talk about this when we talk about judicial review of agency fact-finding, in the next chapter.

The short version: APA Section 706 authorizes courts to set aside agency action or mandate an agency to act, if justified by one of six standards: if that action (or failure to act) is "arbitrary or capricious," unconstitutional, reflective of a misreading of statutory law, procedurally defective, unsupported by "substantial evidence" in the case of a formal agency proceeding, or unwarranted by the facts if those facts are subject to trial *de novo* by the Article III court.

CHAPTER 21

Judicial Review of
Agency Fact-Finding

Judicial review of fact-finding turns mainly on the level of formality of the agency action that produced the agency's fact-findings that are under review. (To repeat a point Chapter 20 made, in a very small category of cases the reviewing court is required to conduct an entirely new trial in the course of finding the relevant facts, under Section 706(2)(F), but this is a category we won't discuss here given its lack of prominence in administrative law today.) If the agency action was formal, then findings made through that formal process are reviewed under the "substantial evidence" standard. If the action was informal, then those findings are reviewed under the "arbitrary and capricious" standard.

We will shortly talk about what this review looks like. But it's important to put on the table a basic question about these two standards: what is the difference between them? Courts are divided on this question. Some judges argue that substantial evidence review is more stringent than review under the arbitrary and capricious standard. This view makes some intuitive sense. After all, formal agency action sounds more elaborate (and indeed, *is* more elaborate) than informal action. Thus, one might conclude that judicial review of that action should be more demanding.

Other judges are more skeptical of this idea. In their view, it asks too much of judges to calibrate their judicial review scales so precisely as to draw a meaningful distinction in terms of stringency between review under these two standards. Instead, these judges suggest that the best way to understand this difference is as it relates to the record to which the agency can resort when defending its decision in court. Note that formal procedures (reviewable under the substantial evidence standard) require that agency conclusions (including fact-findings) be supported solely by the formal trial-type record those procedures generate. *See* Section 556(e) ("The transcript of testimony and exhibits, together with all papers and requests filed in the proceeding, constitutes the exclusive record for decision . . . ."). Thus, some judges argue that the real difference between substantial evidence and arbitrary and capricious review turns on whether the agency can defend its decision by pointing to information that never made it into the public record the agency's procedure generated, with the agency able to do so only when it faces the latter standard. Review under the arbitrary capricious standard allows that evidentiary leniency as a consequence of the agency employing informal procedures— remember that such informal procedures by definition do not create a formal, trial-type record of the agency's proceedings.

Regardless of how that debate is resolved, let's now focus on judicial review of agency fact-finding. It's generally become understood that judicial review of fact-finding essentially entails asking whether a reasonable juror could have found that fact, had the matter been presented to a jury. Indeed, courts have used this standard when applying substantial evidence review, so even if that review is more stringent than fact-finding review under the arbitrary and capricious standard, it still sounds pretty deferential. However, as we will see immediately below, courts will sometimes apply this standard in relatively stringent ways, depending on the nature of the facts at issue and which agency personnel found the facts.

An important question that has arisen in the context of judicial review of fact-finding deals with what a reviewing court should do when different levels of agency decision-makers disagree on the facts. This situation was the subject of a foundational case, *Universal Camera v. National Labor Relations Board*, 340 U.S. 474 (1951). (Ironically, *Universal Camera* was not even an APA case, but the statute in question, the National Labor Relations Act, uses the same "substantial evidence" standard as the APA, and that case has come to be understood as speaking to the meaning of that standard, and the requirement of "whole record" review, in APA cases.)

In *Universal Camera*, the ALJ found that an employee had been fired for legitimate reasons unrelated to his union advocacy. On appeal, however, the agency heads (the "members" of the NLRB) disagreed, and found that the employee had been illegally discharged for his union activities.

The problem this case presented is that, as the last part of Section 706 provided, a reviewing court in this kind of situation was required to review the entire record, including the ALJ's fact-findings that disagreed with the agency heads'. That provision in turn raised the question, how much weight should the ALJ's findings merit on judicial review, in light of the agency heads' contrary findings? In *Universal Camera*, the Court held that the ALJ's findings should be given the "weight . . . they deserve." This might strike you as very unhelpful; however, the Court went on to explain that when an ALJ's finding was based on his determinations of the credibility of the witnesses he heard, that finding should weigh more heavily in the balance. (Such findings are often referred to as based on "primary," or "testimonial" inferences.) This is because only the ALJ actually heard those witnesses testify; by contrast, the agency head only had access to a paper record of what they said. On the other hand, if the ultimate fact-finding (*e.g.*, that the employee was discharged for legitimate reasons) was based on so-called "secondary," or "derivative" inferences, the ALJ's finding merited no special weight. We'll see an example of this latter type of inference in the example below.

Think about how this rule might apply in a given case. If, say, a supervisor testified that the employee had acted in ways that merited termination, and if the ALJ found the supervisor to be a credible witness, the ALJ's ultimate finding in favor of the employer might carry special weight with the reviewing court. On the other hand, consider an observation by the agency heads that the termination occurred two days before a bitterly-contested union election, and a conclusion, based on the agency heads' experience, that terminations so close to a union election almost always tended to be based on the employee's union preferences. That sort of secondary inference would strongly counsel in favor of the agency heads' finding in favor of the employee.

To repeat, this problem arises regardless of whether the agency's fact-findings are reviewed under the substantial evidence or the arbitrary and capricious standard, and regardless of whether one thinks the former is more stringent than the latter. This problem arises in fact-finding review in particular because of the special role of credibility determinations in the finding of facts, and thus, the arguably elevated importance of the trial-level fact-finder (*i.e.*, the ALJ). Of course, whether one finds the primary/secondary inference distinction persuasive depends on whether one believes that trial judges (including ALJs) are good at "spotting a liar" based on how the witness presents herself. This is a highly controversial proposition.

The short version: Most agency fact-findings are reviewed under either the "arbitrary and capricious" or "substantial evidence" standards. While some judges believe that "substantial evidence" review is more stringent than "arbitrary and capricious" review, others believe that the difference between these standards lies only in the ability of the agency to rely on non-public record evidence when defending its findings in court. An ALJ's findings are part of the record that a reviewing court must examine, even when those findings are contradicted by the findings of the agency head on appeal. In such a case, the ALJ's findings may weigh relatively more heavily if they're based on "primary" inferences, that is, inferences drawn from observing live witness testimony.

CHAPTER 22

Judicial Review of Agency Legal Interpretations

Judicial review of how an agency reads its organic statute and other legal materials constitutes an important, but often confusing, part of administrative law. This chapter focuses mainly on agencies' interpretations of statutes, and then concludes with a shorter discussion of agencies' interpretations of their own regulations.

A. Introduction: *Skidmore* and *Chevron*

When a court reviews an agency's interpretation of its organic statute, it will usually apply one of two deference standards: either the one laid out in *Chevron USA v. Natural Resources Defense Council*, 467 U.S. 837 (1984), or the one laid out forty years earlier in *Skidmore v. Swift and Co.*, 323 U.S. 134 (1944). Because *Skidmore* came first, we'll start by discussing it.

The issue in *Skidmore* was what exactly counted as "work" for purposes of the Fair Labor Standards Act, which imposed requirements such as higher pay rates for unusually long working hours. The workers in *Skidmore* were privately-employed fire safety workers who would respond to emergency calls at the employer's plant. Because they were on call for long periods, but periods in which few if any such calls would come in, a question arose whether all of that waiting time, or only part of it, or none of it, counted as work.

When considering this question, the Court took note of an amicus brief the agency had submitted in the case. (The agency did not bring an enforcement action; rather, the claim was brought directly by the workers against the company.) In deciding whether and, if so, how much to defer to the agency's interpretation, the Court noted that Congress had not given the agency the power to promulgate legally binding regulations on this topic. Nevertheless, Congress had authorized the agency to learn about different types of workplaces, and to inform both Congress and the regulated community about the agency's views of how the statute should be applied in various contexts. The agency had done just that, releasing "bulletins" that provided various examples of when it believed that certain types of situations constituted work time for purposes of the statute. The Court concluded that the agency's work in this area had given it valuable expertise that merited respect from a court facing this type of question, even if the agency's answer to a given question was not legally binding.

So understood, the Court in *Skidmore* concluded that the agency's expertise gave it, in the Court's words, "the power to persuade, if lacking the power to control" (*i.e.*, via a binding regulation). But of course, that power to persuade did not just appear automatically. Rather, the Court observed, that "power to persuade" would rise and fall based on considerations such as the consistency of the position the agency had taken, how longstanding that view was, and how thorough the agency had been in its analysis of the given issue.

These *Skidmore* factors make a lot of sense, given the basis of so-called "*Skidmore* deference" in the agency's asserted expertise. Think about a classroom situation: for example, if your professor was constantly correcting the previous things he taught you, he wouldn't have much of a claim to deference based on any sense that he was the expert in the area. Of course, he might merit deference because he was the duly constituted authority in the classroom— we'll discuss that approach to deference when we get to *Chevron*. But for now, you should think about *Skidmore* deference as deference that is grounded in the agency's expertise, which thus helps make persuasive its views on the correct reading of the statute in question.

Chevron deference is different, at least to some degree. In *Chevron*, the Court explained that an agency's statutory interpretations would enjoy deference if they were ultimately grounded in a decision by Congress to delegate to the agency the power to make those interpretive decisions. Thus, *Chevron*, unlike *Skidmore*, is based largely on the notion not of *expertise*, but *authority*—the authority to decide what the statute means. To be sure, *Chevron*, and cases applying it, have also acknowledged the agency's expertise as a reason to defer. But at this very early phase of the discussion, we can draw a conceptual distinction between these two deference standards based on these distinctive notions. As we'll see, this distinction breaks down sometimes. But it's a handy way to conceptualize these two different deference standards, and their implications.

B. What Each Standard Means

As the last section suggested, *Skidmore* deference is based on the idea that an agency's interpretation of its organic statute deserves deference because of the agency's expertise—literally, the interpretation deserves deference because it is likely that the agency interpreted the statute correctly. This understanding of *Skidmore* deference has implications for what that deference standard means.

One major implication of this understanding of *Skidmore* deference is that, despite the "deference" it implies, the court nevertheless makes the final interpretive decision. The only deference the agency gets is deference to the extent the agency is able to persuade the court that the agency likely answered the question correctly. What this implies, in turn, is that the court makes the final decision, which is (again) based on the extent to which the agency persuades the court that the agency's preferred interpretation is in fact the correct one. (Indeed, in one basic sense *Skidmore* "deference" is not really deference at all. If the court "defers" to the agency's interpretation only because it's convinced that that interpretation is correct, then in a real way there's no deference going on.)

This court-centered nature of the interpretive task in turn suggests that there is, in fact, only one "correct" interpretation of the statute. While that idea may seem obvious to you, when we get to *Chevron* deference we'll encounter the concept that a statute can in fact have more than one "correct" interpretation. As we'll see, this difference will constitute a major difference between *Skidmore* and *Chevron* deference, with important implications for administrative law.

So understood, the factors noted as relevant to *Skidmore* deference make good common sense. If the agency's deference claim is based on expertise, then of course it would make sense that the claim would be stronger if, for example, the agency had taken the same interpretive position consistently over a long period of time. Conversely, the claim would naturally be weaker if the agency was always changing its mind.

Chevron deference is different. Because it is based on the authority Congress has given the agency to fill in statutory gaps, the agency's claim to deference does not turn, at least as a conceptual matter, on factors such as the consistency of its interpretation. Indeed, in *Chevron* itself the agency's interpretation, which the Court upheld, had shifted back and forth between the two possible ways of reading the statute.

While *Skidmore* deference simply directs courts to defer to the agency's interpretation to the extent the court is persuaded that the agency likely answered the question correctly, *Chevron* deference has been explained as a formal, two-step process. First, the court determines whether the statute provides a clear answer to the interpretive question. If it does, the court simply gives effect to that clear meaning, without any deference to the agency. But if the statute is not clear, the court proceeds to a second step, in which the court upholds any interpretation the agency offers, as long as that interpretation is reasonable.

Note something important about that second step. That step contemplates a court upholding an agency's interpretation even if the court would have made a different interpretive decision had it been tasked with making that decision independently of any agency interpretation. This is different from *Skidmore*: a court performing *Skidmore* deference ultimately decides for itself what the statute means, even if its decision is aided by a persuasive agency argument. This difference may seem highly theoretical; however, when we explore its implications we'll see that it has significant practical impact.

C. Performing *Chevron*

Because *Chevron* deference is explained as a formalized, two-step process, it's useful to think about what those steps mean in practice—that is, how courts actually perform *Chevron* deference.

Begin with Step 1. The *Chevron* Court stated that courts should use "traditional tools of statutory construction" as part of their Step 1 inquiry into whether the statute clearly answers the interpretive question at issue. You should *not* assume that this direction entails merely a cursory look at the statute to see whether it provides an obviously clear answer. Instead, courts will often engage in a lengthy, careful, and intricate statutory interpretation analysis only to conclude that, indeed, the statute does clearly answer the question, with the result that the court never reaches Step 2.

A prominent example of this type of analysis is *Food and Drug Administration v. Brown & Williamson Tobacco Corp.*, 529 U.S. 120 (2000). That case considered whether the FDA had the power under its organic statute to regulate tobacco. In examining that question, the Court stated that as part of the *Chevron* Step 1 analysis it was appropriate to consider a large variety of what *Chevron* called "traditional tools of statutory construction." The *Brown & Williamson* Court considered the text of the statute, how the provision in question should fit within the regulatory scheme as a whole to create a coherent overall regulatory program, canons of statutory interpretation (that is, general rules of thumb that have been developed to guide statutory interpretation inquiries), how the provision in question ought to be understood in light of other statutes, including those that were enacted later (sometimes many years later), and finally, what the Court called "common sense"— that is, whether it made sense to conclude that Congress would have delegated the interpretive issue in question to the agency instead of answering it itself.

These factors give courts (and litigators) a lot of running room to argue that the statute clearly answers the question at issue, and thus to avoid having to defer to the agency's interpretation under Step 2. Think about some of those factors. Allowing a court to think about how a particular interpretation makes the entire statute "fit together" as a coherent regulatory program authorizes courts to engage in a lot of policy analysis, under the guise of Step 1. So-called "canons" of statutory interpretation are notoriously under-determinative—that is, they allow courts to reach many different conclusions. Indeed, a famous law review article once paired well-known interpretive canons, each of which pointed in the exact opposite direction as its mate. Karl Llewellyn, "Remarks on the Theory of Appellate Decision and the Rules or Canons About How Statutes Are to be Construed," 3 *Vand. L. Rev.* 395 (1950). Similarly, allowing a court to try to harmonize the statutory provision in question with subsequently-enacted legislation allows it to cite an enormous range of material in support of a conclusion that the statute is clear. Finally, the "common sense" that the Court embraces as a final factor of course bestows a great deal of discretion on the court. Taken together, these factors make it clear that Step 1 entails much more than a cursory look at the statutory provision in question.

Step 2 also presents students with challenges. Recall that this step requires courts to uphold any agency statutory interpretation, as long as that interpretation is reasonable. First, Step 2 presents the conceptual question of how an agency interpretation of an ambiguous statute can ever be unreasonable. To put the matter bluntly, how can a law that doesn't answer a particular question nevertheless be clear enough that an agency answer can be rejected as unreasonable? Second, and relatedly, how can a court uphold as reasonable an agency interpretation of a vague statute if, again, we're assuming that the statute has no clear meaning?

One obvious response—that some interpretations, even of unclear statutes, are just clearly wrong—appears promising but runs into problems. Think about this in the context of *Chevron*'s facts. The issue in *Chevron* was the meaning of the term "major stationary source" of pollution. The question was whether that term meant that every smokestack in, for example, a refinery was its own "source," or, as the agency eventually concluded, whether the entire refinery as a unit constituted the source. The Court in that case concluded that the statute was ambiguous with regard to that particular question, and thus reached Step 2 (where it upheld the agency's interpretation).

But consider a counter-factual hypo: what if the agency had interpreted "major stationary source" to include trucks? One might say that this interpretation is unreasonable, and would fail Step 2. Obviously, trucks are not stationary, and so even if the statute was unclear as to the smokestack/refinery issue, an interpretation including trucks as "stationary sources" has to be unreasonable. But is it unreasonable under Step 2, or can we say instead that, as a matter of Step 1, the statute is clear that the statutory term in question excludes mobile sources? On this latter theory, we might say that, while we don't know what the term *means*, we do know what it *does not* mean. If that's how we think about the question, then we're faced with the fact that the interpretive question stops at Step 1. This leaves Step 2 still unexplained.

Given this problem, courts have often explained Step 2 as a requirement that the agency "do its homework"—that is, a requirement that the agency think carefully about the statutory interpretation problem confronting it, and provide a careful, reasoned analysis to the court. As we will see in the next chapter, this approach is very similar to the approach courts take when they review how agencies "make policy"—that is, how they combine the facts they find and the law interpretations they make, and decide on a particular regulatory result. Indeed, the Supreme Court has stated that these two approaches are essentially the same. We'll defer that last point to the discussion of agency policy-making in the next chapter. For now, the important point is to realize that Step 2 of *Chevron* has often been understood to impose this type of "homework" requirement on agencies. When one thinks about it, perhaps this is the best the Court (or anyone else) can come up with when confronted with the oddity of having to determine the reasonableness of an agency interpretation of a statute that, by hypothesis, lacks a clear meaning.

D. When to Apply *Chevron*, and When to Apply *Skidmore*

Chevron was decided in 1984. For nearly twenty years thereafter it was unclear whether a court would apply *Chevron* anytime an agency interpreted a statute, or whether another deference standard would apply in some circumstances. The Court decided this issue in 2001, in *United States v. Mead Corporation*, 533 U.S. 218 (2001). *Mead* dealt with an interpretation of federal tariff laws by the U.S. Customs Service, the agency that regulates the tariffs to be paid on imported goods. The tariff laws are very detailed—they essentially list every tariff category for every type of product that might be imported, and note the tariff federal law requires to be paid on each such product. In *Mead* the agency decided that "day runners"—bound notebooks used for jotting down appointments and short notes—fell under one statutory tariff category as opposed to another.

The issue in *Mead* was whether that tariff categorization merited *Chevron* deference. The Court majority decided that it did not, and that instead it merited whatever deference it deserved under *Skidmore*. *Mead* thus formally resurrected *Skidmore*, whose status had been in doubt after *Chevron*. As discussed below, it thus had the effect of introducing a new, preliminary step into the agency statutory interpretation deference analysis—whether that agency interpretation merited *Chevron* deference, or merely deference under *Skidmore*. Sometimes this new, preliminary step is called "*Chevron* Step Zero."

The *Mead* Court explained that the ultimate question in any issue of this sort was whether Congress intended to grant the agency the power to act "with the force of law." If it did, then the agency merits *Chevron* deference. Note what this "force of law" idea means. As you'll recall, Step 2 of *Chevron* requires courts to uphold any agency reading of an ambiguous statute, as long as that reading is reasonable. That means that, even if the court might have come to a different conclusion on what an unclear statute means, if the agency's contrary reading is reasonable the court has to give it effect. Thus, in a real sense, under *Chevron* Step 2 it's the agency that gets to say what the (ambiguous) statute means, rather than the court. As *Mead* explains, that power flows from Congress, and its decision to grant interpretive authority to the agency.

The question *Mead* addresses is when a court will conclude that Congress did indeed intend to grant that authority to the agency. The Court concluded that a very good indication of such intent is if Congress granted the agency the power to act through a relatively careful process, such as a rulemaking (formal or informal) or a formal adjudication. When Congress did give the agency that power, and when the agency used that power (*i.e.*, when it actually performed a rulemaking or formal adjudication), the Court suggested that it was likely that it (*i.e.*, the Court) would find the requisite congressional intent, and thus apply *Chevron*. For you, this means that a grant of such authority and the agency's use of that authority is a pretty good sign that the court will likely give *Chevron* deference to any agency interpretation that emerges from that rulemaking or formal adjudication. To repeat, the agency has to *use* that authority in order to gain the right to claim *Chevron* deference. For example, it can't just claim *Chevron* deference because it was granted that authority, if the interpretation in question emerged from some other agency process—for example, a policy statement or something even more informal.

But the *Mead* Court went on, and noted that sometimes the Court had declared that *Chevron* was the appropriate deference standard even when the agency did not have or did not utilize rulemaking or formal adjudication authority. A year after *Mead*, in a case called *Barnhart v. Walton*, 535 U.S. 212 (2002), the Court cited a grab-bag of factors that would be relevant to whether or not *Chevron* should apply. The language from *Barnhart* merits a full quotation:

> "In this case, the interstitial nature of the legal question, the related expertise of the Agency, the importance of the question to administration of the statute, the complexity of that administration, and the careful consideration the Agency has given the question over a long period of time all indicate that *Chevron* provides the appropriate legal lens through which to view the legality of the Agency interpretation here at issue."

What does this mean for you? Unfortunately, it means complexity. To be sure, one (relatively) clear rule is that if Congress gives the agency the power to act through a relatively careful process (*i.e.*, rulemaking or formal adjudication) *and* if the agency came up with its interpretive decision in the course of utilizing that authority, then *Chevron* is likely to apply. (Note that informal, notice-and-comment rulemaking counts, for *Mead* purposes, as a type of formalized procedure that usually qualifies the resulting interpretation for *Chevron* deference. But informal adjudication does not, unless the interpretation in question merits *Chevron* deference for some other reason.) On the other hand, if these conditions are not met, that doesn't mean that *Skidmore* necessarily applies. Indeed, as the quote above makes clear, the factors *Barnhart* mentioned can convince the Court to apply *Chevron*.

How does a court actually decide whether a non-rulemaking/ non-formal adjudication process can nevertheless produce legal interpretations that merit *Chevron* deference? Consider *Mead* as an example. The Court in that case observed several things about the customs agency interpretation that it concluded cut against that interpretation meriting *Chevron* deference. The Court noted that the interpretation in question was one that the agency cautioned only applied to products identical to the sample product submitted to the agency. Thus, it had no precedential effect. That decision was also revocable at will, without notice to anyone except to the person who had requested the original customs ruling. Indeed, the agency cautioned other parties *not* to rely on that interpretation. Finally, he noted that these interpretations could issue from any of the 46 ports-of-entry that received imported goods, and that most such interpretations (although not the one at issue in *Mead* itself) contained very little analysis, but consisted mainly of conclusory statements about how the agency had decided to classify the goods in question. The Court concluded that these factors meant that the interpretation in question did not merit *Chevron* deference. Rather, it merited whatever deference was appropriate under *Skidmore*.

Why not *Chevron*? Basically, there seemed to be an undercurrent in the *Mead* opinion that agency interpretations that deserved being treated with the force of law had to be more of what we intuitively think about when we think about law. They had to apply generally (not just to goods identical to the sample submitted to the agency), there had to be some right to rely on how the agency had interpreted the law, including some notice (beyond to the party requesting the initial customs ruling) if the agency wanted to change its mind, and there had to be some reasoning and some central vetting of those interpretations. The Court in *Mead* began its Step Zero analysis by observing that agency legal interpretations come in all shapes and sizes and contexts. The factors *Mead* (and later *Barnhart*) identified as relevant to the Step Zero question seek to explain which of those shapes and sizes and contexts create legal interpretations weighty enough to merit being treated as having the force of law.

E. The *Brand X* Problem

Mead's recognition of two competing deference standards for agency interpretations—*Skidmore* and *Chevron*—introduced complexities into administrative law. First, as already noted, it necessarily meant that now there was a new, "Step Zero" question to ask before performing *Chevron*—the question whether *Chevron* even applied at all. But another problem arose soon after *Mead* and *Barnhart*, which was resolved in *National Cable & Telecommunications Ass'n v. Brand X Internet Services*, 545 U.S. 967 (2005).

Brand X raised the following type of problem. The story starts when an agency's statutory interpretation is challenged, and the court concludes that that interpretation merits only *Skidmore* deference. The reviewing court applying *Skidmore* concludes that the agency's interpretation is incorrect, and thus rules against the agency. Then, at some future point, the agency acts in a way (say, via a rulemaking) that merits *Chevron* deference, and re-states its earlier view of what the statute means (the view that the court rejected). When that latter case comes to that very same court (say, a particular geographic federal circuit court) the agency claims *Chevron* deference for its interpretation.

What's the problem? On the one hand, the earlier judicial decision applying *Skidmore* deference constitutes the conclusive view of that court on what the statute means. Don't forget that under *Skidmore* it's the court that has the authority to make the final interpretive decision, even if that decision is aided by an expert agency, and, indeed, even if the court ends up persuaded that the agency's view is correct. Thus, this would suggest that the subsequent agency action would not have an impact on the court's view of what that statute means, since, again, the first court had decided the issue conclusively in that jurisdiction.

On the other hand, the agency's subsequent statutory interpretation still merits *Chevron* deference, based on the conclusion (derived from *Mead* and *Chevron* itself) that the agency has been given the authority to make the interpretive decision, as long as it's reasonable. This would thus suggest that it has the right to go to court and claim the authority to interpret the statute, even if the earlier court decision had decided that interpretive issue and had done so seemingly conclusively (subject only to the court overruling itself, as an *en banc* court can do to a federal appellate panel, or as the Supreme Court can do).

In *Brand X* the Court resolved this conundrum in the following way. It told courts in the position of the second, subsequent court in this example essentially to read the original court's opinion. If that earlier opinion had concluded that the statute gave a clear answer to the question at issue, then the second court was directed to reaffirm that earlier court's interpretation. But if that earlier opinion had concluded that the statute was ambiguous, and that the court simply disagreed with how the agency had resolved the ambiguity, then the second court was directed to defer to the agency's current reading, as long as that reading was reasonable.

If this approach sounds familiar, it should. The direction the Court gave to courts in this situation was essentially to read *Chevron* back into the first opinion, and essentially to determine what that original court would have said if it had applied *Chevron*. While this might seem a logical resolution to this problem, it also raises the prospect that the agency in that second lawsuit could effectively overrule what purported to be the conclusive decision of the Article III court in the first opinion. Don't forget that *Skidmore* deference contemplates the court making the final decision on what the statute means. The *Brand X* resolution means, however, that the agency in the subsequent litigation can get what it wants if it satisfies *Chevron* Step 2, even if what it wants is a ruling contrary to what the original court handed down.

This oddity reflects the real-world problems that arise when two deference standards, with two different roles for Article III courts, co-exist. To be sure, to the extent *Chevron* and *Skidmore* deference look similar and lead to similar results, the disruptiveness caused by the existence of two deference standards becomes less extreme. Nevertheless, it remains a real issue.

F. The Future of *Chevron*

It has long been assumed that *Chevron* is a foundational case and that, regardless of any ambiguity about when it applies or what it means in practice, it would remain a central part of administrative law. In recent years, though, the Court has grown more hesitant about even considering whether to apply *Chevron* in any given case, and individual justices have criticized it as inconsistent with courts' role in interpreting law. In future years, it is quite possible the Court will consider whether to formally overrule it. If it does, it is an open question what would take its place: a broader embrace of *Skidmore*, an abandonment of all deference doctrines, or something else entirely.

G. *Auer/Seminole Rock* Deference

So far, this chapter has discussed the deference due to an agency's interpretations of its organic statute. But what about an agency's interpretations of its own regulations? It's very common for agencies to have to interpret their own regulations. If those regulations implement a complex statutory scheme, they can themselves be quite complex and in need of interpretation or clarification. Thus, it often happens that agencies interpret their own regulations.

When an agency interprets its own regulations it gets a large amount of deference. The foundational case for this proposition is *Bowles v. Seminole Rock & Sand Co.*, 325 U.S. 410 (1945), which the Court followed in another important case, *Auer v. Robbins*, 519 U.S. 452 (1997). Hence, this sort of deference is often referred to as "*Auer*" deference or "*Seminole Rock*" deference. Again, under this standard the agency enjoys a lot of deference: as the Court stated in both of these cases, an agency's interpretation of its own regulation will be upheld unless it is "plainly erroneous or inconsistent with the regulation."

There is great logic in deferring to an agency's interpretations of its own regulations. Clearly, the agency itself is in the best position to know what its own regulations mean; after all, it wrote those regulations. Conversely, it might be odd for a reviewing court to tell an agency that the agency has misread its own regulation. On the other hand, the existence of this distinct level of deference raises the possibility for confusion, just as with *Brand X*, discussed earlier. For example, until 2006, agencies were able to promulgate a regulation that essentially repeated or, in the Court's words, "parroted" the statute, and then "interpret" that regulation and claim *Auer* deference. Note the trick here: the parroting regulation would quite likely prevail on *Chevron* review. In turn, when the agency interpreted that regulation, it would essentially be interpreting the statute (since both the statute and the regulation say the same things and indeed use the same words). Thus, the agency would be able to claim *Auer* deference for what is essentially an interpretation of the statute.

The Court put a halt to this practice in *Gonzalez v. Oregon*, 546 U.S. 243 (2006), refusing to grant *Auer* deference to agency interpretations of such "parroting" regulations. But similar opportunities continue to exist for agency gamesmanship. For example, an agency could promulgate a very vague regulation interpreting a statute. Such a vague regulation might well survive *Chevron* review exactly because it could not be shown to be unreasonable since it was so vague. But then the agency could interpret that vague regulation in any way it liked (given how vague the regulation is) and again claim *Auer* deference.

Given these issues, and also given the increased judicial resistance to deferring to legal interpretations generally (as discussed in the prior section), *Auer* deference has become controversial. In 2019, a bare five-justice Supreme Court majority reaffirmed *Auer*, but imposed substantial limits on when such courts would accord such deference. In *Kisor v. Wilkie*, 139 S.Ct. 2400 (2019), the Court remanded a case to the lower court that had accorded *Auer* deference to an agency interpretation of its own regulation, to consider whether that interpretation truly merited such deference. The Court enunciated a list of factors that courts should consider before according *Auer* deference, including whether the regulation was truly ambiguous and whether the agency's interpretation was sufficiently authoritative and based in its expertise to justify deference. This analysis makes clear that in the future courts will not accord *Auer* deference automatically or even easily.

The short version: Agency legal interpretations will be reviewed based on either *Skidmore* or *Chevron* deference. *Skidmore* deference requires reviewing courts to defer to the agency's interpretation of its organic statute to the extent the court is persuaded that the agency likely answered that question correctly, based on indicators of the agency's likely expertise on that question. *Chevron* requires that courts give effect to the clear meaning of a statute, but if the statute does not have a clear meaning on the relevant question they must defer to any reasonable agency interpretation. The *Mead* case requires courts to decide the *Skidmore* versus *Chevron* question based on the court's decision whether Congress intended the agency to have the power to act with the force of law; if the court concludes that Congress did have that intent, then it will apply *Chevron*. The *Seminole Rock* and *Auer* cases require that courts give a great deal of deference to agencies' interpretations of their own regulations. In recent years the Court has shown discomfort with *Auer* deference. Indeed, some justices have also objected to *Chevron* deference.

CHAPTER 23

Judicial Review of Agency Policy-Making

In addition to finding facts and interpreting law, a critical function that agencies perform when they act is making policy. Unlike fact-finding and law-interpreting, though, policy-making is not an obvious concept. For administrative law purposes, policy-making can be understood as combining facts and law to reach a regulatory result. For example, an agency tasked with workplace safety might find the fact that a particular machine is dangerous to use and costs very little to replace. It might then interpret its organic statute as authorizing it to prohibit "unreasonably dangerous workplace conditions." Filtering the facts that it finds through the law that it interprets, the agency might then conclude, as a policy matter, to promulgate a regulation banning the use of that machine.

This very simple example should make it clear that policy-making includes several steps. As we'll see, the foundational Supreme Court case addressing judicial review of policy-making requires the agency to take two steps, which can be further sub-divided into a series of criteria for judging that policy decision. We begin, though, with a reminder of what Section 706 says about judicial review of agency action, and how its requirements apply to policy-making.

Recall from Chapter 20's brief tour of Section 706 that that section authorizes courts to mandate or set aside agency action in six situations. Recall also that, of those six reasons the court can give for its decision, two of them—the "substantial evidence" requirement and the "arbitrary and capricious" requirement—focus on agency action in general, rather than on particular types of actions (such as law interpretations or procedural actions the agency takes). These two default standards apply to, among other things, policy-making. Substantial evidence applies when that policy-making is the result of a formal process. The arbitrary and capricious standard applies when policy-making is the result of an informal process, such as an informal notice-and-comment rulemaking. Recall Chapter 21's discussion of the debate among courts about whether these two standards require different levels of judicial scrutiny of agency action, or, instead, whether those two different standards simply require different things from the agency in terms of the record on which the agency action has to stand or fall when it is challenged in court. That discussion from Chapter 21, which dealt with agency fact-finding, also applies to courts' use of these two standards in the policy-making context.

Standards of review aside, it's important to consider what the agency is doing when it engages in policy-making. As one might expect, the nature of that policy-making function influences what judicial review of that function looks like. For that reason, consider what an agency is doing when it makes policy, as in the simple example we used to start this chapter. An agency tasked with regulating a topic such as workplace safety has to learn the facts about that subject—things like, which machines and practices are dangerous, and how expensive and difficult it would be to require industry to improve conditions. The agency also needs to understand what it is required, authorized, and not allowed to do under its organic statute. Most relevantly for our current purposes, it would have to put those facts and that law together to reach a regulatory result—as in our example, banning a particular machine.

This understanding of the policy-making function leads us to how courts have described judicial review of that function. The most important statement of what that judicial review entails comes from a Supreme Court case, *Motor Vehicle Manufacturers Ass'n v. State Farm Mutual Insurance Co.*, 463 U.S. 29 (1983). *State Farm* involved a decision by the agency responsible for automobile safety to rescind a regulation that required carmakers to install so-called "passive restraints"—that is, either automatic seat belts or airbags. We'll see in a moment how the Court reviewed that decision. But for current purposes the important thing is what the Court said about what judicial review of that policy decision entails. The Court explained that such review requires courts to examine, first, whether the agency "considered the relevant factors" the statute instructed it to consider and, second, whether in doing so the agency committed "a clear error of judgment."

Before considering these requirements in more detail, stop and think about what these requirements suggest. In addition to finding the relevant facts and understanding its mandate under the law, the agency must now actually apply that law that it (presumably) correctly understands—that is, it must "consider the relevant [statutory] factors"—and, second, it has to do so reasonably—that is, it may not make "a clear error of judgment." Leaving fact-finding aside for the moment, one can thus combine the law-interpreting and policy-making functions into a three-step process, which requires the agency (1) to interpret the statute correctly, (2) do what that correct interpretation requires it to do, and (3) be reasonable in doing so. But keep in mind that the first step of this process is judged under the standards discussed in the previous chapter.

Consider now how the Court fleshed out these two policy-making requirements and applied them in *State Farm*. As noted earlier, the issue in *State Farm* consisted of the agency's decision to revoke an auto safety regulation that had required carmakers to install either automatic seat belts or airbags in all new cars by a certain date. While the original regulation contemplated that carmakers would comply with a combination of seat belts and airbags (that is, installing automatic seat belts in some cars and airbags in other cars), at some point it became clear to the agency that carmakers were planning on complying almost entirely by installing automatic seat belts. This frustrated the agency, which had hoped that carmakers would gradually install airbags in cars, and thus introduce that new and promising safety technology to the American people. That frustration, as well as other considerations, led the agency to rescind the rule.

The Court struck down the rescission, on the ground that it was arbitrary and capricious. The Court began by amplifying on the two-part test set forth earlier—that the agency must consider the relevant statutory factors and that it not commit a clear error of judgment. It wrote, "Normally, an agency rule would be arbitrary and capricious if the agency has relied on factors which Congress has not intended it to consider, entirely failed to consider an important aspect of the problem, offered an explanation for its decision that runs counter to the evidence before the agency, or is so implausible that it could not be ascribed to a difference in view or the product of agency expertise."

Importantly, the Court reminded readers that the agency's decision had to stand or fall on the explanation it provided when it made the decision—after the fact explanations, for example, by the agency's lawyers on judicial review, would not do. This is an important difference between review of agency action under the arbitrary and capricious standard, and judicial review of legislation under the "rational basis" standard of the Equal Protection and Due Process Clauses. "Arbitrary and capricious" sounds vaguely like "rational basis," but it's very important that you keep these concepts distinct.

The Court concluded that the agency's rescission failed arbitrary and capricious review. First, it faulted the agency's failure even to consider amending the rule to require carmakers to install airbags in some cars, after learning that they were not otherwise planning on complying with the existing requirement via airbags. The Court did not fault the agency for failing to amend the regulation in this way; rather, the problem was that the record failed to indicate that the agency even considered that option. One can easily see this as a failure "to consider an important aspect of the problem."

The Court then reviewed the agency's thinking about the value of seat belts. (Recall that it was the carmakers' decision to comply with the existing regulation almost exclusively through seat belts that led the agency to rescind the regulation as, essentially, not worth the expense.) The agency had in front of it the results of a study, in which some consumers voluntarily purchased cars with automatic but detachable seat belts (that is, seatbelts that, although detachable, come from the factory attached and remained so until the user unbuckled them). That data did indeed show an increase in seat belt usage. Nevertheless, the agency stated that it could not reliably predict a meaningful overall increase in seat belt usage based on this data, given that this group of consumers could be expected to be very safety conscious (after all, they had voluntarily spent additional money for the automatic seat belts). If even that group experienced only a modest increase in usage, the agency reasoned, there was no reason to think there would be a significant increase in usage among the broader population.

The Court rejected this reasoning. It cited the fact that the factor of inertia (*i.e.*, the fact that automatic belts came attached, and required an affirmative effort to detach) to conclude that "there would seem to be grounds to believe that seatbelt use by occasional users will be substantially increased by the detachable passive belts."

Finally, the Court criticized the agency's views about *non-detachable* automatic belts—that is, belts that could not be unbuckled. The agency considered such belts, but as lumped together with examples of what it called "use-compelling features," which it concluded might complicate drivers' and passengers' exits after an accident, and which it suggested would trigger public disapproval given widespread fears about being trapped in a car after an accident. The Court noted that the agency had previously accepted a carmaker's assurance that these belts in fact allowed easy exit from the car in the case of a collision, and that the agency had not explicitly renounced that conclusion. It also found arbitrary and capricious the agency's decision to lump this option together with other possible safety features, including those that in the past had proven to be highly unpopular.

Note one important thing about what this review looks like. Essentially, *State Farm* faulted the agency for not doing its regulatory homework carefully enough—for example, by not considering an "airbags only" option and (in the Court's view) misreading the data the agency received from the study sample of drivers who purchased cars with automatic seatbelts. If the concept of the agency "doing its homework carefully" sounds familiar, it should. Recall from the previous chapter that when the Court in *Chevron* explained what Step 2 review would look like—that is, what judicial review of an agency interpretation of an ambiguous statute would look like—it basically said that it would look like an inquiry into whether the agency had thought about the interpretive issue carefully. Thus, judicial review of an agency's statutory interpretation under Step 2 of *Chevron* has often been thought of as very similar, if not essentially the same thing, as judicial review of agency policy-making. *See, e.g., Judulang v. Holder*, 565 U.S. 42 (2011) (remarking on the similarity of *Chevron* Step 2 and policy-making review).

This careful consideration of *State Farm* is necessary because the case has become so important in judicial review of policy-making. It's hard to fault the Court when it struck down the agency's failure to consider an "airbags only" option. Given both the agency's hope to see airbags introduced into the market and the carmakers' plans to comply with the existing regulation almost entirely by using seat belts, it's easy to see why the Court found it arbitrary for the agency to fail even to consider requiring some installation of airbags.

On the other hand, the Court's treatment of the seat belt issue is notable for the degree to which it was willing to second-guess the agency. (To be sure, this part of the opinion only gained 5 votes, while the discussion of the airbags-only option was unanimous; still, there was a majority for this part of the opinion as well.) The intrusiveness of the Court's review has been understood as a warning to agencies to ensure that their regulatory analyses are detailed and respond to every possible major objection. Indeed, lower court cases both before and after *State Farm* have come to describe the type of review they perform when they review agency policy-making as "hard look" review. Strikingly, early uses of this phrase (from the early 1970s) suggested that the court's job was to ensure that the agency had taken a "hard look" at its regulatory options, but by the end of the decade, the meaning had changed to the point that courts were describing their job as taking a "hard look" themselves at the agency's analysis. That's a subtle but very significant difference. *State Farm* is a good example of this latter, more stringent understanding of hard look review.

Such review is controversial. Of course, incentivizing agencies to be careful is a good thing. On the other hand, lawyers, judges, and scholars have worried that this sort of careful insistence on the agency getting things exactly right has slowed down agency action and made it more expensive. This is something that your professor might be interested in discussing in class.

The short version: Policy-making can be understood as the agency's combination of fact and law into a regulatory result. Courts review agencies' policy-making either under the "arbitrary and capricious" standard (for policy decisions reached after an informal process) or the "substantial evidence" standard (for policy decisions reached after a formal process). The same ambiguity about the difference between these standards that was discussed in Chapter 21 exists here as well. Regardless of the standard applied, such review requires that the agency have (1) considered the factors the organic statute requires the agency to consider and (2) not made a clear error of judgment. Often, this type of review can be quite stringent, as is illustrated in *State Farm*'s critique of the agency's analysis of the safety benefits of automatic seatbelts.

* * * * *

THE TAKEAWAY

What are the main issues this Part addresses?

- **What courts are authorized to do when they reach the merits of a lawsuit challenging agency action.**

  Courts are authorized to compel an agency to act, or to set aside an agency action, when one of six conditions set forth in APA Section 706 is satisfied.

- **The judicial role in reviewing agency fact-finding.**

  For the most part, agency fact-finding is reviewed under either the "arbitrary and capricious" standard (if the facts were found in an informal agency proceeding) or the "substantial evidence" standard (if the facts were found in a formal agency proceeding).

- **The role of the ALJ's fact-findings when the agency head disagrees with those findings.**

  As part of the record of the case, an ALJ's findings must be considered by the reviewing court. If the ALJ's findings were based on his observation of witnesses, then those findings weigh relatively more heavily than if his findings were based on secondary, or derivative, inferences.

- **The judicial role in reviewing an agency's interpretation of its organic statute.**

  Agency statutory interpretations are reviewed under either the *Skidmore* standard or the *Chevron* standard. A court will employ the *Chevron* standard if it concludes that Congress intended for the agency's interpretations to have the force of law; otherwise, it will employ *Skidmore*.

- **The judicial role in review an agency's policy-making.**

  Agency policy-making decisions will be reviewed based on either the "arbitrary and capricious" standard (if the decision resulted from an informal agency proceeding) or the "substantial evidence" standard (if the decision resulted from a formal agency proceeding). Either way, such review seeks to ensure that the agency considered the factors the organic statute required it to consider and that, when it did, it did not commit a clear error of judgment.

PART SIX

Agencies and Information

As you're likely well-aware, in today's world information is critical to power and influence. Administrative agencies possess vast amounts of information—data and studies that agencies themselves generate, as well as information they collect from persons, either informally or via a legal requirement.

This final Part of this *Guide* considers the relationship between agencies and information. It begins, in Chapter 24, by examining agencies' power to *gather* information, if necessary by compulsion. It then considers, in Chapter 25, their obligation to *disclose* information they possess, under the requirements of the Freedom of Information Act. As these chapters make clear, agencies have a great deal of power to gather information, but they also face significant obligations to disclose the information they have.

CHAPTER 24

Agency Authority to Compel Production of Information

Agencies are authorized to collect a vast amount of information from private parties. For example, an environmental statute may require polluters to submit data about their emissions, or a regulation of cosmetics may require the producer to submit information about the chemicals used in the product. Often, private parties furnish this information more or less willingly. But when they don't, agencies have significant power to compel parties to produce it.

A. The General Rules

The breadth of the power described above might make you wonder whether it implicates the Fourth Amendment, which bans "unreasonable searches and seizures" and requires "probable cause" in order for the government to obtain a search warrant. When an agency issues an administrative subpoena for business records, the Supreme Court has held that the Fourth Amendment imposes fewer obstacles than in the traditional criminal context, given the long history of legislative provisions requiring corporations to maintain records open to public and government scrutiny. *Oklahoma Press Pub. Co. v. Walling*, 327 U.S. 186 (1946). The theory, then, is that the private party has relatively weaker privacy interests in this context and the government, through its statutory obligations to implement whatever regulatory scheme is prompting the subpoena, has strong interests. Indeed, four years after *Oklahoma Press*, the Court analogized an agency's investigative power to that of a grand jury, and stated that an agency otherwise acting properly can demand information simply on suspicion of a statutory violation or even to confirm that there is no such violation. *United States v. Morton Salt Co.*, 338 U.S. 632 (1950).

This is not to say that agencies are thus free to demand any information, under any circumstances. First, the agency's investigation must be authorized by law. This is usually not a difficult hurdle, as long as the agency is investigating conduct that plausibly appears to come within the agency's regulatory jurisdiction. Indeed, often the information the agency is seeking will be understood as relevant to the agency's determination of whether, in fact, it has regulatory authority over the conduct it is investigating; in such cases courts will generally allow the agency to proceed with the subpoena. *See, e.g., Equal Employment Opportunity Commission v. Sidley Austin Brown & Wood*, 315 F.3d 696 (7th Cir. 2002). Courts may also inquire into whether the subpoena is reasonably specific and not unduly burdensome. In considering this issue, the Court in *Oklahoma Press* cautioned that the reasonableness of the subpoena's specificity would naturally vary with the nature of the inquiry, such that, for example, a broad-ranging inquiry might reasonably trigger a broad-ranging subpoena. Claims of burdensomeness are often rejected by courts if the agency offers protections, such as protective orders, that ensure that proprietary information handed over to the government is not then disclosed publicly. (On this point, see Chapter 25, which discusses an exemption from the Freedom of Information Act's disclosure mandate for such proprietary information.) In addition, the information sought must not be privileged in some way. *See, e.g., Upjohn Co. v. United States,* 449 U.S. 383 (1981) (allowing a taxpayer to assert attorney-client and work-product privileges in response to an IRS summons).

B. Physical Inspections and Searches

Of course, the Fourth Amendment is addressed to more than document production requests. It is also—perhaps even primarily— addressed to physical intrusions and searches by government agents. Such intrusions and searches can apply in administrative law, as well: for example, an agency regulating food safety may wish to inspect or even search a food production facility to ensure that it is clean and unlikely to produce tainted food.

The Supreme Court's jurisprudence in this area has followed an unsteady path. In *Frank v. Maryland,* 359 U.S. 360 (1959), the Court held that a health inspector did not need a search warrant to enter a house in search of the source of a rodent infestation in the neighborhood, given the historic acceptance of such searches and the strong public interest in sanitation. But in *Camara v. Municipal Court,* 387 U.S. 523 (1967) and *See v. Seattle,* 387 U.S. 541 (1967), the Court rejected this view, and imposed a general warrant requirement for administrative searches. However, the Court in *Camara* cautioned that such warrants did not need to satisfy the traditional legal standard of probable cause. The Court in *See* (which dealt with a search of a commercial warehouse) also left open the possibility that warrants would not be required if the business in question required a license which in turn was granted on the condition of the applicant's consent to warrantless searches. It applied this idea in two cases, *Colonnade Catering Corp. v. United States,* 397 U.S. 72 (1970) (dealing with a licensed retail liquor establishment) and *United States v. Biswell*, 406 U.S. 311 (1972) (dealing with a licensed firearms dealer).

However, in *Marshall v. Barlow's, Inc.*, 436 U.S. 307 (1978), the Court rejected a surprise inspection by the Occupational and Safety Health Administration (OSHA), despite OSHA's argument that such inspections were necessary in order to ensure worker protection. Instead, the Court limited *Colonnade* and *Biswell* to situations where the target of the inspection was part of a "pervasively regulated" industry that had been subject to a "long tradition of close supervision."

In later cases, though, the Court gave a broad interpretation to the concept of a "pervasively regulated" industry, including within it the mining industry, *Donovan v. Dewey*, 452 U.S. 594 (1981), and the auto dismantling business, *New York v. Burger*, 482 U.S. 692 (1981), even though, in the context of *Burger*, the regulation did not appear particularly pervasive. However, most recently, in *City of Los Angeles v. Patel*, 576 U.S. 409 (2015), the Court refused to include within the group of "pervasively regulated" industries the operation of a hotel. Thus, it rejected a municipal code provision that required hotel operators to provide police with specified information about their guests, upon the police's warrantless demand.

Aside from its obvious unsteadiness, this jurisprudence reflects the difficult balancing the Court feels compelled to do in the context of administrative searches. On the one hand, such searches are deeply problematic as a matter of constitutional law, and, as the Court suggested in *Camara*, it would be ironic if the only persons who could count on the Fourth Amendment's protections are those suspected of criminal wrongdoing, as opposed to those suspected of mere civil infractions. On the other hand, there is good reason to allow agencies a great deal of latitude in carrying out their complex regulatory duties, which usually carry with them something less than the threat of criminal liability.

C. Self-Incrimination

The Fifth Amendment, which states that no person "shall be compelled in any criminal case to be a witness against himself," is also relevant to administrative information-gathering. Of course, to implicate this protection the sanction in question must be criminal, rather than civil. Moreover, the privilege can only be asserted by a natural person, not a corporation. Indeed, a business's custodian of records—a natural person—must turn over the business's documents even if those documents would incriminate the custodian herself, since in that case the custodian is deemed to be acting for the corporation. *Braswell v. United States*, 487 U.S. 99 (1988).

The nature of a particular act of document production as "compelled" also suggests significant agency power to compel production despite the Fifth Amendment. For example, a third party (say, an accountant) can be required to produce documents that implicate the third party's client (say, a taxpayer), since the target of the investigation (the taxpayer) is not being compelled to produce anything. *See Couch v. United States*, 409 U.S. 322 (1973). Similarly, the taxpayer in this type of situation could be required to produce documents her accountant prepared, even if those documents implicated the taxpayer, since they were not the utterances of the taxpayer herself. *See Fisher v. United States*, 425 U.S. 391 (1976).

Another important limitation on the non-self-incrimination right is the so-called "required records doctrine." Under this doctrine, the right is not violated when an agency compels the production of records an individual keeps for a business when that record-keeping is itself mandated by law. In such a case, the records are considered "public records" and the individual is considered a custodian of such records, such that the subpoena does not necessary infringe the Fifth Amendment right. *See, e.g., Shapiro v. United States*, 335 U.S. 1 (1948) (applying this doctrine to a businessperson who was ordered to produce the sales records that he was legally required to maintain).

While this doctrine remains good law, it does not apply when the records-maintenance requirement, instead of being imposed in "an essentially non-criminal and regulatory area of activity," is directed at a "selective group inherently suspect of criminal activities." *Marchetti v. United States*, 390 U.S. 39 (1968). For example, in *Marchetti*, the document maintenance requirement consisted of a requirement that bookmakers report information about their activities to the Internal Revenue Service as part of a tax on the occupation of bookmaking, even though bookmaking was illegal under federal and state laws. The theory here is that the information-submission obligation essentially traps bookmakers into either admitting that they are violating the law or violating the information submission requirement itself. By contrast, in a case like *Shapiro*, where the information-submission requirement appears merely regulatory, the businessperson's legally-compelled maintenance of those records—records of legal activity—does not necessarily place him in the same kind of trap when he is compelled, under the required records doctrine, to produce those records.

The short version: Administrative searches are subject to the Fourth Amendment, although the precise rules governing such searches are different than those normally applied to Fourth Amendment issues. In particular, the Amendment's requirements are relaxed for "pervasively regulated" businesses. Similarly, while the Fifth Amendment's protection against self-incrimination applies to agency document demands, the Court has decided cases that allow agencies significant latitude to demand incriminating documents from persons or their agents.

CHAPTER 25

Freedom of Information

Federal law provides persons significant rights to access government information. While the original version of the APA included some provisions speaking to information access, many of the current rights to such information derive from the Freedom of Information Act (FOIA), *codified at* 5 U.S.C. § 552, enacted in 1966 and amended several times since then. For simplicity, this *Guide* refers to all of these provisions as "FOIA."

A. Self-Executing Disclosure Requirements

FOIA has several main components. Section 552(a)(1) requires an agency to "make available to the public" the following information:

> "(A) descriptions of its central and field organization and the established places at which, the employees (and in the case of a uniformed service, the members) from whom, and the methods whereby, the public may obtain information, make submittals or requests, or obtain decisions;

(B) statements of the general course and method by which its functions are channeled and determined, including the nature and requirements of all formal and informal procedures available;

(C) rules of procedure, descriptions of forms available or the places at which forms may be obtained, and instructions as to the scope and contents of all papers, reports, or examinations;

(D) substantive rules of general applicability adopted as authorized by law, and statements of general policy or interpretations of general applicability formulated and adopted by the agency; and

(E) each amendment, revision, or repeal of the foregoing."

Some of these types of documents should sound familiar to you, most notably agencies' "rules of procedure," (a)(1)(C), and "substantive rules of general applicability adopted as authorized by law, and statements of general policy or interpretations of general applicability formulated and adopted by the agency," (a)(1)(D). These documents, of course, constitute the types of rules that are either required to be promulgated only after a rulemaking process (whether informal or formal), or those that Section 553 explicitly exempts from that rulemaking process. (See Chapter 6 for a discussion of the rulemaking process, and Chapter 7 for a discussion of the types of rules that are exempt from that process.) More generally, Section 552(a)(1) seeks to ensure that the public knows how to access the agency and what processes the agency has in place for performing its various functions.

Subsection (a)(2) requires agencies to "make available for public inspection in an electronic format" a variety of other types of documents, including all opinions in agency adjudications, staff manuals "that affect a member of the public," and records that have been released to other persons subject to subsection (a)(3). (Subsection (a)(3) is discussed immediately below.)

B. Disclosure in Response to Document Requests

Subsection (a)(3)(A) is in many ways the core of FOIA. It requires that:

> "Except with respect to the records made available under paragraphs (1) and (2) of this subsection [discussed immediately above], and except as provided in subparagraph (E) [discussed immediately below], each agency, upon any request for records which (i) reasonably describes such records and (ii) is made in accordance with published rules stating the time, place, fees (if any), and procedures to be followed, shall make the records promptly available to any person."

Thus, this subsection requires agencies to turn over any "records" as long as (1) the requester "reasonably describes" them, (2) the requester follows the agencies' rules regarding procedures and fees for such requests, (3) the records are not otherwise required to be disclosed under subsections (a)(1) and (a)(2), and (4) the records do not fall under either one of the exceptions FOIA specifies in subsection (a)(3)(E) or elsewhere in the statute. (As you'll see, most of the exceptions appear not in subsection (a)(3)(E) but, in fact, in a completely different subsection of Section 552.)

This is a very powerful requirement. There is no limit on the motives that a person may have for requesting documents. To be sure, as we'll see, some motivations, such as to obtain a competitor's trade secrets, are implicitly disfavored by means of one or more exemptions. But FOIA is not limited to requests made by public interest groups for public interest reasons. For example, in *U.S. Dept. of Justice v. Tax Analysts*, 492 U.S. 136 (1989), the Supreme Court upheld a FOIA request, made to the Tax Division of the Department of Justice, for copies of all federal court tax opinions the agency had on file, by a for-profit firm that produced a newsletter on tax law. Despite the obvious fact that the requester was essentially using the agency as a shortcut in its information-gathering, the Court concluded that FOIA was not limited to requests (or requesters) who were acting in the public interest. (As we'll see, though, FOIA does allow the agency to reduce its fees if the request promotes the public interest.) Indeed, the Court also held that rejecting the request was improper even though the records in question—the federal court opinions on tax matters—were publicly available elsewhere.

C. Documents Exempted from FOIA Requests

As one might immediately suspect, such a broad right of information access cannot come without exceptions. Obvious concerns—among others, about privacy, national security, trade secret information, and the prejudicing of ongoing government investigations—suggest that there have to be limits on the government's obligation to turn over any information someone may request. And, indeed, FOIA provides a list of nine exceptions to that access right in Section 552(b). But before we get to those exceptions, we need to mention an exception that appears earlier, in Section 552(a)(3)(E). Subsection (a)(3)(E) reads as follows:

> "An agency, or part of an agency, that is an element of the intelligence community (as that term is defined in section 3(4) of the National Security Act of 1947) shall not make any record available under this paragraph to—

(i)   any government entity, other than a State, territory, commonwealth, or district of the United States, or any subdivision thereof; or

(ii)   a representative of a government entity described in clause (i)."

This exception states the common-sense rule that an intelligence agency shall not make available any requested information to a foreign government or its representative.

In addition to this exception, Section 552(b) provides a list of nine exceptions, which can be summarized (or sometimes directly quoted) as follows. These exceptions authorize the non-disclosure of information that is:

1.   authorized by an executive order to be kept secret for national security reasons;

2.   "related solely to the internal personnel rules and practices of an agency;"

3.   specifically exempted from disclosure by another statute;

4.   "trade secrets and commercial or financial information obtained from a person and privileged or confidential;"

5.   "inter-agency or intra-agency memorandums or letters that would not be available by law to a party other than an agency in litigation with the agency, provided that the deliberative process privilege shall not apply to records created 25 years or more before the date on which the records were requested;"

6.   personnel and medical files and similar files the disclosure of which would constitute a clearly unwarranted invasion of personal privacy;

7. "records or information compiled for law enforcement purposes, but only to the extent that the production of such law enforcement records or information (A) could reasonably be expected to interfere with enforcement proceedings, (B) would deprive a person of a right to a fair trial or an impartial adjudication, (C) could reasonably be expected to constitute an unwarranted invasion of personal privacy, (D) could reasonably be expected to disclose the identity of a confidential source . . ., (E) would disclose techniques and procedures for law enforcement investigations or prosecutions . . ., or (F) could reasonably be expected to endanger the life or physical safety of any individual;"

8. reports prepared by bank examiners; or

9. geological and geophysical information "concerning wells."

Many of these exemptions are complex, or at least not fully self-explanatory. For example, Exemption 5 preserves for an agency the same evidentiary privileges it would have if it was in litigation. While this seems straightforward—for example, exempting a government attorney's work-product from disclosure—this exemption leads to odd results when it's combined with earlier FOIA provisions' requirements that the agency disclose the reasoning for decisions it makes. For example, in *NLRB v. Sears, Roebuck & Co.*, 421 U.S. 132 (1975), the Court had to consider a FOIA request for NLRB memoranda concerning the agency's decisions whether or not to bring enforcement actions against employers who had been accused of violating federal labor law. The Court concluded that if those memos explained why the agency had decided *not* to sue, they had to be disclosed, since such memos constituted the reasoning behind a final agency decision. But if those memos explained why the agency had in fact decided to sue, they were exempt, since the litigation would then be proceeding and the memo in question could easily be understood as containing the agency's theory of the case.

Other exemptions can be similarly intricate. For example, consider Exemption 4, which covers "trade secrets and commercial or financial information obtained from a person and privileged or confidential." In *Critical Mass Energy Project v. NRC*, 975 F.2d 871 (D.C. Cir. 1992) (*en banc*), the appellate court concluded that Exemption 4 was designed in part to ensure voluntary cooperation from private parties who were asked to turn over sensitive information, by ensuring that such information would not become the subject of a FOIA request. Thus, according to the court, information would less likely be considered "confidential" (and thus protected from disclosure) if the original possessor had been *required* to turn it over to the government. While this analysis is logical, it's not an intuitive understanding of what constitutes "confidential" information. In addition, the exemption's inclusion of "trade secrets" as exempted information effectively incorporates into FOIA the tangled law governing what constitutes a "trade secret."

Consider also Exemptions 6 and 7, both of which implicate personal privacy concerns. Exemption 6 exempts from FOIA "personnel and medical files and similar files the disclosure of which would constitute a clearly unwarranted invasion of personal privacy," while the relevant part of Exemption 7 exempts "records or information compiled for law enforcement purposes, but only to the extent that the production of such law enforcement records or information . . . (C) could reasonably be expected to constitute an unwarranted invasion of personal privacy . . . ." Exemption 7's concern for personal privacy clearly strikes the disclosure-privacy balance more in favor of privacy/non-disclosure, as compared with

Exemption 6. Presumably, Exemption 7's criminal investigation focus motivated this additional concern for privacy.

The rest of Exemption 7 gives other law enforcement investigation-based reasons for withholding requested information. Consistent with what we said above about that exemption's personal privacy provision, the rest of Exemption 7 is also often read broadly. For example, it's been held to apply in cases where an investigation is "reasonably anticipated." *Sussman v. U.S. Marshals Service*, 494 F.3d 1106 (D.C. Cir. 2007). It's also been understood to apply not just to criminal matters, but to civil and regulatory cases as well. *Pope v. U.S.*, 599 F.2d 1383 (5th Cir. 1979).

D. "Reverse FOIA"

One issue that arose in FOIA litigation is whether FOIA's exceptions are mandatory, in the sense that an agency is not authorized to disclose information that falls within them, even if it voluntarily chooses to do so. In other words, the argument arose that if FOIA *allows* an agency to withhold a particular piece of requested information, then it is *required* to withhold it. In *Chrysler Corp. v. Brown*, 441 U.S. 281 (1979), the Court rejected that argument, reasoning that FOIA was a disclosure statute, not a secrecy statute that mandated keeping the exempted information private. However, the Court noted that other statutes may in fact mandate the confidentiality of certain information. For example, the Trade Secrets Act, 18 U.S.C. § 1905, prohibits the federal government from disclosing information that is a trade secret. Thus, a decision by an agency not to invoke Exemption 4's trade secrets exemption but instead to disclose such information might be subject to challenge as a violation of the Trade Secrets Act. In a post-*Brown* case, the D.C. Circuit held that the Trade Secrets Act's coverage is as broad as Exemption 4's coverage; thus, a trade secret that an agency *may* withhold under Exemption 4 is also therefore information that an agency *must* withhold under the Trade Secrets Act. *CNA Financial Corp. v. Donovan*, 830 F.2d 1132 (D.C. Cir. 1987).

E. Fees

Recall that FOIA generally does not distinguish between types of requesters—*i.e.*, requests made for commercial reasons are generally treated the same as those made for public interest reasons. One exception to this rule concerns fees. FOIA provides that "fees shall be limited to reasonable standard charges for document *search, duplication, and review*, when records are requested for commercial use." 5 U.S.C. § 552(a)(4)(ii)(I) (emphasis added). However, it also provides that "fees shall be limited to reasonable standard charges for document *duplication* when records are not sought for commercial use and the request is made by an educational or noncommercial scientific institution, whose purpose is scholarly or scientific research; or a representative of the news media." *Id.* § 552(a)(4)(ii)(II) (emphasis added). Moreover, it specifies that "Documents shall be furnished without any charge or at a charge reduced below the fees established under clause (ii) [*i.e.*, the two provisions quoted earlier in this paragraph] if disclosure of the information is in the public interest because it is likely to contribute significantly to public understanding of the operations or activities of the government and is not primarily in the commercial interest of the requester." Thus, FOIA favors non-commercial requests regarding the fees the agency is authorized to charge and the fee waivers the agency is authorized to grant.

F. Judicial Review

A disappointed FOIA requester may seek judicial review of the agency's failure to respond to the request as the requester wished. The court's review is *de novo*, and FOIA places the burden on the government to justify the exclusion. FOIA also authorizes the judge to review the withheld documents *in camera* (that is, privately in chambers) to determine whether the agency's position is well-taken.

The short version: FOIA gives persons broad rights to request documents and information possessed by the federal government. Such rights are not limited to persons acting in the public interest; even persons acting for business reasons may request documents. However, all document requests are subject to a list of exceptions, which include exceptions for national security, privacy, and protection of confidential information. Just because a document falls under one of FOIA's exceptions does not mean that the agency is thereby legally prohibited from disclosing it, unless some other federal law affirmatively prohibits such disclosure.

* * * * *

THE TAKEAWAY

What are the main issues this Part addresses?

- **The power agencies have to compel the production of documents and to engage in searches.**

   Even though agencies are subject to the Fourth and Fifth Amendments, they nevertheless enjoy significant power to engage in searches and compel the production of documents. In particular, Fourth Amendment warrant requirements standards are adjusted to account for the distinct context of administrative searches.

- **Agencies' obligations to disclose information they possess.**

   The Freedom of Information Act (FOIA) imposes significant obligations on agencies to disclose information requested by private parties. Those obligations are subject to a series of intricate exceptions.

Concluding Thoughts and Advice

Administrative law is complex, as you've no doubt realized by this point. Even this *Short and Happy Guide* gets pretty intricate at times. That complexity is in some ways inevitable: it's complicated enough designing a bureaucratic structure for institutions that administer something as complex as the federal government, let alone designing a legal structure to control that bureaucracy and keep it within the guardrails established in the Constitution.

Still, there are ways to cut through some of the complexity. Now that you've worked your way through the semester and through this *Guide*, look back and take a broader perspective on what you've learned.

1. In a basic way, administrative law is about *administrative process* (rulemaking and adjudication, covered in Parts Two and Three of this *Guide*) and *judicial review of the results agencies come up with* (Part Four examines when and on what terms that review is available, while Part Five considers what that review looks like). Why

237

rulemaking and adjudication? Because that's what governments do when they impose legal requirements: they legislate (or, in the agency context, they promulgate regulations) and they adjudicate (whether via a court system or an administrative adjudication system).

2.   The Constitution speaks to many parts of this process. As noted in the first paragraph of this conclusion, the Constitution establishes some basic guardrails governing the role of agencies in our constitutional structure (Part One's consideration of the non-delegation doctrine, agency adjudicative power, and presidential control over agency personnel). The Constitution also speaks to the administrative process—after all, it's called the Due *Process* Clause for a reason. Hence, Chapter 13 deals with due process, and Chapters 8 and 14 consider what due process demands in terms of agency procedures free of *ex parte* contacts and unfair bias.

3.   Article III also has a lot to say about administrative law. Article III-based concerns drive much of standing doctrine (Chapter 17) and at least some of the timing issues you studied in Chapter 19. More generally, the institutional role of federal courts as guarantors of government legality influences the presumption of reviewability that you studied in Chapter 16.

4.   But the administrative state is also heavily connected to Congress and the President. That's why we study Congress's ability to grant agencies legislative power (Chapter 1) and adjudicative power (Chapter 2). It's also why the Court insisted in

Vermont Yankee that courts could not impose more procedures on agencies than those Congress has chosen to require, either in the APA or the agency's organic statute (Chapter 6). But if Congress wants to exert control over agencies it has to do so through constitutionally-allowed mechanisms—which don't include legislative vetoes (Chapter 4).

5. The President is, of course, a key player as well. That's why he has at least some Article II-based right to control the tenure of officials who help him carry out his constitutional responsibility to execute the law (Chapter 3). It also explains why presidents since the 1980s have required agencies to consult with the White House on regulatory matters (Chapter 9).

6. As we said in Part Six, today more than ever information is a critical element of power and influence. That's why it's so important that agencies have both great latitude to gather information (Chapter 24) and significant obligations to share information when a member of public requests it (Chapter 25).

Of course, these simple observations of how the material fits together along different axes don't make that material any easier to grasp. It's still hard. But take a moment every so often—and in particular, toward the end of the semester when you're trying to put everything together—and try to see not just the individual trees but the entire forest. If you do that, then you will start mastering not just the details, but the overall thrust, of this incredibly important part of American law. I hope this *Guide* has helped at least a little in your quest for that mastery.

Good luck!